In a Year of Our Lord

In a Year of Our Lord

A Memoir of American Innocence

by JOHN MULLEN

ARBOR HOUSE *New York*

To my wife Frances

Contents

In a Year of Our Lord

Where Did You Get That Hat?

Where did you get that hat...
Where did you get that title?
Isn't it a nobby one...
And just the proper style?
I should like to have one
Just the same as that!
Where'er I go they shout...Hello!
Where did you get that hat?

As a former child I consider myself somewhat of an authority on juvenile matters at the turn of the century, particularly the Golden Year of our Lord, 1912, when I was nine and most of the incidents recalled here took place.

I don't know how it is today, but young citizens in my time lived a life on two levels; distinct, yet closely related: the world of one's peers against a backdrop of the adult world comprising one's family, the grownups of one's noisy neighborhood and the oftimes peculiar carryings-on of all oldsters generally.

Whether you accepted it or not (and at times I didn't) you were part of the family, and whether or not you were concerned, the joys, sorrows, defeats, conflicts or victories of that family were branded on your sensitive young soul because your elders loved you and if necessary would beat your arse until you got the message. So, in self-defense, you developed the emotional technique of participating in family affairs by standing carefully on the perimeters, observing the ridiculous antics of the adults but at the same time avoiding direct involvement.

My mother and her teenaged sister Bess were beautiful women—mother in a sort of sedate hair-in-a-bun fashion, and my young aunt endowed with the sort of gorgeousness that was known to cause a horse-pulled trolley to come to a lurching stop as the conductor leered at Bess while she daintily crossed against traffic. She was just nineteen, ten years my senior and often referred to in family circles as "Pretty Bess," a nickname that annoyed her. Of course, I worshipped her

4

and was madly in love. I think she felt the impact of my passion, and in an impish way would often flirt with me. She was what is known as "black Irish," medium tall, full bosomed, ivory-cream skin, near-black curly hair to her shoulders, and blue-violet eyes. She sang in a throaty blues style and made her living as a pop singer selling ten-cent song sheets in a Philadelphia "Five and Dime." And what songs! *You* hum them today. A few examples of popular tunes written and sung all over the nation in 1912: "Frankie and Johnny," "Dear Old Girl," "When I Lost You," "Love's Old Sweet Song," "When Irish Eyes Are Smiling," "Turkey Trot," "A Little Love, a Little Kiss," "I Want a Little Lovin' Sometimes," to name a few.

Pretty Bess knew them all, and according to family legend she sang through thirty-two titles one busy Saturday afternoon at the Five and Dime. Although she had the song sheets at her finger tips, she only fluffed twice, quickly recovered and went right on without reading either music or lyrics. Song sheets for piano sold in huge volume during the early years of the century. This was all before radio, "talkies," or, of course, television. Singing was a national pastime—soloists, quartets or choirs. People sang whether they could or not. Americans had a surprising affinity to the song—in almost any shape or form—popular ballads, ragtime, choral, minstrel or just plain bellowing in the corner bar or on a river barge, or on a moonlight excursion down the Delaware. And the demand brought forth the supply; from around 1900 to 1920 over a thousand titles appeared, many to live on to become American classics.

Uncle Mike loved Pretty Bess' voice but he swore he would put an end to her "standin' exposed and singin' to a pack o' leerin' scalawags who should have better to do than hang around the Five n' Dime listenin' to a minor female sing her pretty heart out!"

Uncle Mike was my father's brother as Bess was my

mother's sister ... it was years later that I learned all uncles need not be the father's brothers and all aunts not females of my mother's family. Anyhow, Bess and Mike met at my parents' wedding. Met. And separated. And did not meet again until Bess was grown and gorgeous and Mike cursed himself for not having noticed her sooner. "But better late than never, my lad...."

It is true about Adam and that Apple. I know. My own fall from grace took place when I was nine ... because of a beautiful woman's desire for feathers!

My descent into the Pits of Sin resulted from a conversation I overheard in our kitchen one Sunday when my beautiful young aunt came down by trolley car from Philadelphia for her weekly visit to our family in Chester. She was out of sorts and even cool toward me, which was unusual.

"Now, Bess," Mother said. "What is it? Aren't you feeling well?"

"I'm all right, sis."

"I know better ... something's bothering you...." She saw me standing at the door and exploded. "Out!"

I sauntered to the parlor, hit the piano keys a few licks, then stole quietly back, for I, too, didn't like to see my usually ebullient aunt in a sad mood. I heard the continued conversation between the sisters:

"... it's just that I *know* I'll look great..." Bess was saying.

"You'll *not* be a hussy just to please that foolish audience ... I won't have it!" Mother was quiet but firm.

"An ostrich feather *doesn't* make a hussy, and anyhow I can't afford five whole dollars. That's a week's wages."

I determined then and there that my Aunt Bess would get her ostrich-feathered hat. With wonderful self-confidence she planned to win the local amateur talent contest at the

Nickelodeon and eventually defeat the best talent in the Philadelphia area in the grand finale at the Orpheum. She wanted the hat badly. I brooded, discarded several flamboyant fund-raising schemes such as heavily bandaging my six-year-old brother Frank and placing him prominently under the great town lamp on Market Square with a sign reading: "Please Help A Injured Child." I finally realized that gathering the enormous sum of five dollars would have to be in nickles, dimes and quarters ... then I decided that we must raid the Pickle Works!

I throbbed with Sacrifice ... this time we would not merely fill our bellies, we would sell the pickles to Murphy's bar! (Saloons in those days offered ample free lunch along with the drinks.) Our opportunity occurred a few days later and caused no end of grief to me—and to the Katz family next door.

The houses on our street were identical brick affairs with two stone steps leading to the front door and so close to the gutter that it was possible to lean out the parlor window and converse freely with anyone on the sidewalk. Thus we knew each other well, we knew each other's innermost secrets ... and even I, at the age of nine, was aware that the Katz family, like most immigrants in the 1900's, was constantly in trouble. Not the petty anxieties that beset most of the neighborhood, but trouble that pelted down in disastrous proportions as it was to do in the affair of the Pickle Works.

First among the Katzes there was Davey. Even at the age of seven, he had all the qualities for success. He was aggressive, shrewd, and a thief at heart. Then there was Mr. Katz. Daily at noon he brought his junk wagon to the front of his home, tied a canvas feed bag on Becky and then went in for his meal of an onion, a slice of homemade corn bread and a smoked whitefish. Becky was perpetually hungry. As a junkman, Mr. Katz had difficulty making ends meet and he was inclined to be sparing with the oats. On several occasions

Becky had stuck her straw-hatted head through the parlor window and shattered the pane to convey the fact that she was still unsatisfied. Once she dragged the wagon onto the sidewalk and kicked the front door off its hinges, neighing loudly all the while. Mr. Katz rushed out with more oats; after that Mrs. Katz kept the window raised and the door open.

In addition to Davey, there were four other Katzes: Uncle Jake, who made schnapps in the cellar for religious purposes; Davey's older brother, Moisha; Mr. Katz and his wife, a frail woman with stunned eyes. She cooked, scrubbed, worried . . . and coped, miraculously, with three goats Uncle Jake kept tethered in the backyard. He treasured the creatures for the health-giving quality of their milk, and as companions, for Uncle Jake was as mean-tempered as his charges and none of the neighbors would speak to him. He worked in a nearby forge shop which made axheads. Mrs. Katz was perhaps more troubled by the goats than by any other problem of her complex existence, for all the women hung their wash in the tiny backyards—they laundered twice weekly to keep up with the sanitary needs of their broods—and it was a sad sight to see her struggle to devise ways of hanging the larger stuff—bed sheets and such—beyond reach of the goats. Uncle Jake would come home for lunch, encrusted with soot. For the sake of his pets he would wash his grimy hands before trying to milk them. He never succeeded, for the animals disliked *him* intensely.

The morning of the Pickle Works Affair, when we got to school it was closed and placarded by the Board of Health because two children had become ill with diphtheria. We greeted the news with enthusiasm. The weather was the sort only children really feel and smell, an invigorating odor of horse manure in the breeze and the mild winter air saturated with the soft brackish oyster odor of the nearby Delaware River. (Old Adam, too, must have been restless on such a

day.) Dutifully, we reported home—if we hadn't we would
have been clobbered (a sure sign of maternal affection in our
circle) and after a stern warning to keep out of trouble we
promptly headed for the back alley to figure out what sort
of constructive endeavor we might devise this glorious day.
Our alley was a long one and ran the entire length of the
street. A high board fence separated the rear of the houses
from the Pickle Works (as everybody called the establish-
ment), a big livery stable run by Old Man Armitage, and up
at the far end, the Quaker churchyard. All three institutions,
the Pickle Works, the horse haven and the saintly Quakers
found it expedient and necessary to barricade themselves
from us. We, however, had long ago solved the problem of
circumventing the high fence by digging a tunnel beneath it
that was kept camouflaged on either side with carefully laid
boards.

After a quick consultation I decided that Moisha, Davey,
my younger brother Frank and I would make one of our infrequent sorties on the Pickle Works (nothing, I decided was
too dangerous in the service of good Aunt Bess and her de-
voutly desired ostrich-feathered hat). In the yard of the
works, protected by the roof of an open shed, was an immense wooden vat about twelve feet high where thousands
of juicy cucumbers soaked in salt brine in the process of
becoming pickles. The brine was covered with a thick mat-
ting of dill, caraway seed and other emphatically odored
condiments. The company also stored materials in the yard,
including huge demijohns of concentrated ammonia. We had
but one objective in mind when we squirmed under the
fence. The great pickle vat. Caution was necessary—extreme
caution—since we had already created a mild scandal some
months before. Six of us, the additions being Hank Webster
and Nez Knowles, had raided the joint on a Sunday, broken
into the building and taken off with a supply of jarred mar-
malade, various jellies and copious quantities of rubbery half-

treated pickles. Several hours later after consuming this mess, six nauseated kids retired to their homes, green-faced, shiny with cold perspiration, marks of recent regurgitation on blouse fronts.

The shocked cries of our frightened mothers, who thought we had somehow been fatally poisoned, echoed around the corner to the proprietor of the Pickle Works—who lived in a *nice* house. He immediately investigated and swore out a warrant for our arrest. Our families, poor to begin with and ill affording it, promptly paid off.

This morning, therefore, fully conscious of being one-time losers, we planned to pull our raid on the vat with calculated care. Like most kids of that age, we had a code of seniority. The older always let the younger stick their necks out first. Otherwise the younger ones weren't permitted to consort with their betters. So, in this instance, my brother Frank, being six, and Davey Katz, only seven, had to bow to Moisha's and my nine years. Frank squirmed through the tunnel, and when nobody booted him out I followed and Moisha came after me. Davey was last, his job being that of lookout. We saw Davey's dark, curly head come through, but that was as far as he got. He let forth a surprised shriek as someone on the other side yanked him back. We stared at the hole mutely. Next we heard a high-pitched flow of angry Yiddish and recognized Mrs. Katz' voice. I turned to Moisha.

"What did your mother yell at us?"

"Aw, she called us names and said she'll tear my heart out whin I git home, that's all." Then, without warning, we found ourselves trapped. Four factory hands came out. We dove for cover behind a stack of crates before they saw us. We held our breath. The men went about the job of transporting big wooden pails of pickles from the vat into the building. A heavy ladder leaned against the vat, and one of the employees scooped out pickles with a wire net contraption. He filled the pails and passed them down. Two men sat and loafed while the other pair labored. We couldn't duck back through the fence without being seen and probably caught. We had entered the yard about eleven in the morning and for the next hour we accomplished the virtually impossible for kids of our age. We kept quiet.

Shortly before noon the workmen knocked off, and with sighs of weary relief we prepared for action. The last man disappeared through the door when we were up and at it. By this time we had a desire for those pickles amounting to a maniacal compulsion. I don't think I've had a yen so intense in my life, for pickles, or for anything else. I directed Moisha to go up the ladder and throw the prizes down to me. He climbed the ladder. My brother Frank wandered idly among the crates, loyally awaiting instructions. He had a peculiar and infuriating habit in those days; he simply had to *smell* anything he couldn't identify from his six years of living. To him the world was full of exciting and/or shocking odors. So Moisha ascended the ladder while Frank nosed around, peeked into crates and sniffed. Moisha hissed to get my attention, and I deduced from his sign-language that the pickles were too far down for his reach. Usually the vat was filled to the brim, but those workmen had taken out dozens of pails. I turned to find a piece of wire for Moisha to snag the pickles with and casually glanced at Frank, who was in the act of pulling a rubber stopper out of a demijohn of pure ammonia. Before I could warn him—I dared not yell—he stooped, took a deep sniff and promptly keeled over backward, knocked-out cold. His body, cushioned with copious layers of baby fat, hit the ground with a soft thud. I was stunned. Surely, he was dead. I looked up to get Moisha's help in the sudden, tragic passing of my brother. To my surprise, Moisha was no longer on the ladder. I blinked and pondered. I knew Moisha *hadn't* come down. Instantly the impact of double disaster hit me full force. There was only one place Moisha could be at that moment. *In the pickle vat.*

He had leaned over too far and fallen in. I was torn with indecision. My own flesh and blood was lying a few feet away in the morning sun, his plump little face composed in what I believed was cherubic departure from this world, while Moisha was up to his eyebrows in pickles. And I knew he couldn't swim a stroke. But *he* was alive, for I could hear weird gurgling sounds in the big vat. I scooted up the ladder. Moisha was thrashing about as fat pickles bobbed around him, his hair matted with dillweed. His face, as it alternately rose and disappeared, looked peculiarly like someone with a bad case of measles, for the caraway seed covered him from crown to neck. I made a frantic grab and got a handful of sticky hair. I held on. Moisha was half drowned, saturated outside and internally with pickle brine. Somehow, I helped him climb over the vat rim, and my gasping, very sick associate-in-crime came down the ladder and finally reached land. He gazed at me in consternation, began to stutter, and the biggest bubble I've ever seen before or since slowly formed on his lips. I watched it closely as he fell straight back in a dead faint. I left him and ran to my brother Frank, who, I saw, wasn't deceased at all, only stunned and emerging from a blackout. I got him to his feet. In a dreamy sort of daze he started again for the big demijohn, probably to take another sniff. To him, this was the *prize smell* of his experience. A *lulu*. He didn't seem to recognize me.

I now faced the difficult task of getting them both under the fence. Frank was out of this world, and Moisha was out cold. With considerable persuasion I managed to get Frank through the fence, then dragging the unconscious Moisha (who smelled to high heaven), I shoved his inert feet through. Frank stood rigidly in a daze on the other side, and I couldn't make him understand I wanted him to drag Moisha out. I did the next best thing—I squirmed through, reached in and grabbed Moisha by the heels. I had him halfway through when all hell broke loose. His mother, feeding the goats in her backyard, looked over the fence, saw us, and with an agonized scream rushed into the alley, her cries of despair arousing every mother within earshot as she dragged Moisha's sodden and apparently lifeless form from the tunnel. I received a hefty clout on the ear. By now my mother had joined the throng and had found Frank in his rigid trance. Events reached a Homeric climax as Mr. Katz drove his straw-hatted and hungry Becky to the front of the house and Uncle Jake entered the backyard to attempt to milk his uncooperative goats. And a swarm of wholesale produce market workers came up the street on their way to a local restaurant for lunch.

Word of disaster had a lightning quality in our sort of neighborhood. About a dozen men hurried into the alley to give a hand to a kid, who, they heard, had just been fished out of the Delaware. Now, the third house down from ours and next to the Katzes' was tenanted by a crotchety old woman known as Widow Dubrowski. She rarely associated with the other women, constantly complained about us kids. That very day she had received a tall, gold-decorated statue of the Virgin Mary. Precisely at noon, a few moments after it was delivered, Widow Dubrowski had proudly placed the statue smack in front of her parlor window for the whole neighborhood to see and envy.

Meanwhile, back in the alley, Mrs. Katz battled the well-meaning market workers who had to fight her off in order to apply artificial respiration to Moisha's pickled form. At the same time his father, hearing the news, dropped Becky's feed bag and ran frantically to the alley. Becky fumed. She kicked in all directions, shied up the sidewalk until she stood in front of Widow Dubrowski's house. As the houses were identical, Becky apparently must have brooded a while, hanging her straw-hatted head and perhaps thinking bitterly of the cruelty of man. Then, by whatever reasoning a horse uses, Becky seemed to recall she had gotten immediate results in the oats department simply by shoving her head through the window, glass and all. Which Becky now did— except it was Widow Dubrowski's place. And there, in pristine newness, was the statue of the Virgin Mary. It toppled. It fell. It shattered.

Now Davey, whom Mrs. Katz had locked in the cellar, got into the act. Davey had sampled his Uncle Jake's bootleg brew, found it a strange new taste to his liking, and while Moisha, Frank and I were up to our depredations in the Pickle Works, Davey had gotten himself thoroughly plastered. On hearing the bedlam in the back alley where the market workers were giving Moisha a real workout, taking turns sitting on his frail belly and pumping his arms—Davey climbed through the cellar window and staggered off. A few minutes later he appeared at the end of the alley, lurching wildly and singing a high soprano song he had learned from his Uncle Jake—which, naturally, was a ribald number and never intended for mixed company.

My mother, all this time, had me gripped painfully by one ear, as she cooed to Frank, who was slowly emerging from his trance. Mrs. Katz wailed with joy when Moisha grunted, fluttered his eyes and once again gave forth with a beautiful bubble; at which point Mr. Katz, in tears and biting his knuckles, spotted Davey. So did his mother. Everyone in the crowded alley seemed to become aware of Davey at that precise instant. A deep hush fell over the throng. Davey weaved his way toward us, giving forth with his Yiddish folk song. Moisha came to. His father fainted. My mother observed the prone Mr. Katz.

"Ahh ... the poor, poor man," she sighed. Then *bam!* I was fetched another clout on the ear. The produce clerks turned their ministrations on the father. I was yanked into the house whammed fore and aft and sent upstairs forever. Slowly the neighborhood settled down to a mild uproar, which was normal, except that a policeman came and served a warrant on poor Mr. Katz. The widow Dubrowski had charged him with the destruction of the Virgin Mary.

And upstairs I cogitated on the Cruelties of Parents, Mankind in general and the fact that my aunt's ostrich feathers, the pursuit of which had started the whole thing, would have to wait.

CHAPTER II

Take Back Your Gold

Take back your gold
for gold can never buy me,
Take back your bribe
and promise you'll be true,
Give me the love,
the love that you'd deny me,
Make me your wife
That's all I ask of you.

PRETTY BESS' HAT was still on my mind—and my conscience.

By dint of my superior wit and natural inclination to felony I could accumulate five cents a week—the only kid in the neighborhood with the ante for admission to the local movie house, the Nickelodeon. On many occasions the five cents admission got me and my six-year-old brother Frank into the show after long, tiresome arguments with the ticket seller in which I loudly claimed Frank was only 3¼ and tall for his age. All children four years and under were admitted free if accompanied by a parent. On that sticky point I said loudly that we were parentless and therefore poor, helpless and cruelly put-upon orphans, and usually at that point the ticket seller (Old Man Baer, who also doubled as projectionist when the movie began) would savagely shove the ticket toward me whereupon Frank and I would casually saunter in. That nickle on many occasions not only got my brother and me into the Nickelodeon, but also Moisha and Davey Katz, Nez Knowles, and Hank Webster, the latter two also members of my gang, who every Saturday waited at the side fire exit door for me or some other community-minded young citizen to open the door from the inside, whereupon the gang literally rushed in and dove into the laps of the nearest customers. That amounted to six for a nickle—not such a bad deal at all.

Every Saturday morning, glorious hot sunshine with a briny high tide, or crystalled streets of snow, I had to sit with pencil and lined writing pad (Mother's bright idea of

18

bolstering my reluctance to do school homework) and the following monologue generally occurred:

Mother: Five pounds sugar ... let's see how we are on flour ... yes ... five of flour and *bulk* out of barrel, mind you, none of that packaged Pillsbury-two-cents-more. They must think we're made of money—and yes, young man, black molasses ... and take this pail along for a pound of sweet butter ... and ...

It always began that way, and the week's meat and grocery list included, generally, a five pound roast of beef, about the same in pork, a two-pound bag of fresh-ground coffee (grinding and revelling in the gorgeous odor was one of the jobs I *liked*), a three or four pound shad or smaller fresh mackerel, and occasionally a goody like a pound of brown sugar for her baking. Provisions such as eggs, vegetables and milk were bought directly from the Mennonites who farmed the outskirts on acreages my father claimed a man could almost eat off'n, the farms were so tidy and clean. Their beautifully groomed horses and hex-marked wagons came every Friday morning. Anyhow, I would eventually scrawl the shopping list which would include sufficient provender for a household twice our size, and my mother would give me a five-dollar bill.

"Now mind you don't lose the change!"

Nobody ever heard of allowances in my neighborhood, you earned your pennies or that nickle by whatever honest or dishonest means available. If you hung around the nearby fish or fruit and vegetable stalls (the merchants bought and sold from the farmers—except the Mennonites) or fishing vessels that plied the Delaware and the bay on a commission basis, you could pick up an occasional dime for delivering something. Shoppers could buy a heaped bushel basket of lucious juice-oozing peaches for a quarter. Or you could walk down the markets to Goff's Fish and Oysters and pick up a

fat shad for fifteen cents. If you were from the better part
of town you could take home a pound of Delaware sturgeon
roe for thirty-five cents. You brought your own wooden
basket and *shoveled* it full of big fat juicy Delaware Bay
oysters for one dollar. Or you could stand at the rough plank
table along the entire wall of Goff's and eat yourself silly
from fresh-shelled oysters or clams with hot Baltimore sauce
for another quarter. The reason that was so expensive was
because a leather aproned shucker opened the bivalves as fast
as you could put them down. All the town drunks could be
found lined up at the busy planks of any Saturday morning,
sipping clam juice (on the house) as they waited their turn.

My little red wagon and I generally took a full hour to
make the few blocks from the neighborhood to Austin's Provisions in the teeming shopping area on lower Market Street.
It always took a good ten minutes to fight my way past the
candy store. The delicious aromas therefrom were demoraliz-
ing and conducive to a weak will giving rise to fantasies of
breaking-and-entering at night or a bold daylight armed rob-
bery with bloodshed if necessary. The candy store man
would eventually tire of my heartbreaking visage and come
to the door, vowing:

"You just getta hell along or I kick your skinny ass!" or
words to that effect with a thick Swiss accent. He claimed to
a customer who asked him why he was so stern: "Dem damn
kitts dirty my clean vindow wit' dere dirty wet noses!" After
my weekly odor-orgy at the candy store window I would
always linger a while at Schiller's Ice Cream Parlor. More
excruciatingly lovely odors. While inhaling, eyes shut, various flavors (chocolate, strawberry, peach, pineapple, vanilla—
enrapturously endless flavor variations—*tasted* through my
nose!) I dawdled another ten minutes or so, and instead of
nose running, it now became chin-dripping saliva—a trick
exclusively mastered by nine-year-old window-gazing veterans. My next stop was Monk's Bicycle and Household Ma-

chine Repairs ("Sodering, [sic] Parts Replaced") where I lolled at the ten-speed bike racer and won the World Champion Riding-Backward-a-Mile-a-Minute Gold Medal. Finally I got to Austin's, did my shopping, swallowed three giant finger scoops of peanut butter out of the open keg, downed a big briny pickle in four gulps, and filled my pockets with hickory nuts.

Mr. Austin finally said: "If you're through, sonny, give this to Mother." He handed me my scrawled list with the price appended beside each item, also the accurate weight if it ran a little above or below the mark. For instance, the five-pound roast beef now read: "5½ lbs.... total 47¢."

It was that list that enabled me to indulge my perfidious talent every Saturday. By simply adding one cent to five different items—for instance, I penciled in 48¢ on the roast beef —I came up eventually with a pilfered nickel for the Nickelodeon. That meant a whole afternoon ... two movies, maybe a Pearl White mayhem series, a new but very funny little man with a tiny mustache, a cane and derby ... and once a month, a tremendous stage show—"Amateur Tryouts." Every Saturday I meant to save that nickle for Bess' hat. But consider it: I was not a free agent ... my whole gang depended on me. I was beset by responsibility ... so, I went to the Nickelodeon.

Besides the Nickelodeon, Mr. Baer also owned a dry goods store. He worked every day except Thursday and Saturday in the store to try to cover his losses at the Nickelodeon, which he opened and ran in those two days while his wife and daughter handled the dry goods emporium in his absence. Mr. Baer, unfortunately, was a born loser, and no man ever worked harder at that goal.

When the final ticket was sold, Mr. Baer closed the window, ran in and tried to subdue the foot stomping, hooting audience, then ran up and started the projector, which always broke down twice or thrice each show. The audience,

child to adult, would rise to its collective feet and bellow
mockery and obscenities while old Baer nervously got the
projector to run again, often with a sharp clacking sound that
would, after some few minutes, bring the madding crowd
back into vehement action. The monthly amateur night invariably ended in noisy fistfights among the various relatives
and friends of the contending aspirants. Police Chief Mc-
Cluskey repeatedly warned Old Man Baer he would close the
house unless the customers were more circumspect.

It was this brawl that my Aunt Bess wanted to win. Talent
she had . . . and beauty . . . and determination, but no ostrich-
feathered hat. My soul fried in guilt. Secret guilt, because the
sole adult male to whom I could turn, my father, had his own
problems just now.

By all the usual standards of judgment, Father was a fairly
reasonable man, most certainly he was kind and generous . . .
but despite good health and a strong physique, all his life he
suffered from a severe case of rigid convictions. And when he
felt called upon to retort with what he fondly called his cold,
lashing logic (his definition, exclusively) he was a hard man
to back against the wall. Often, he felt it his duty to exercise
his reasoning powers upon his two younger brothers, who
usually were up to something that didn't make good sense.
My Uncle Aloysius, for instance, who lived over in New
Jersey, once whipped himself up to a crusading lather and
announced he was going to abandon his trade as a stereotyper
with the Curtis Publishing Company and throw in his lot
with a group of Irish intellectuals who intended to buy an
island in the Bahamas, set up a communistic colony and
thenceforth dedicate their efforts to overthrowing the entire
British Empire *and* the Pope. Father turned *his* intellectual
powers loose on that family crisis and maneuvered Uncle
Aloysius into the arms of a devout Irish girl who in very
short order had him happily married and diapering several
squalling newborns without a whimper.

But Uncle Mike refused to succumb to Father's logic. He was tired of hauling kegs of beer, he declared; furthermore he would go to the Klondike and come back with enough virgin gold nuggets to elevate the whole damn family to the fancy lace curtain status.

Uncle Mike would sit with a bottle of ale in front of him, his solid heavy body rigid with stubbornness, his black hair neatly combed, and hear my father out. Father would get angry because no one, Uncle Mike especially, could apparently understand his profound grasp on the state of the world and what it portended for the future of all mankind. A well-read man, he was firmly convinced that the world had nearly reached its peak in social, economic and scientific development.

Father would say slowly: "If it's barrels of gold ye want, stay here, Michael, and somehow we'll get you set in a business. It'll take longer that way, but there's money to be made in a sensible fashion."

"All right, Sandy," Uncle Mike invariably countered. "Call me a fool or a scatterbrain . . . but it's gambler's blood I have in me."

"And I don't want to see me own kind's blood splattered over a barren country," Father would bark. "Look man, we came along too late, jist a few years too late for th' frontier! It's gone! And don't expect to find it up in Alaska either."

"Ha, hear 'im now!"

Father would ignore him. "The world's changed almost overnight, what with science and invention and one thing and another." He motioned to the silvery gas mantel glowing on the wall. "In another year or two, every house will have thim Edison electric lamps."

Usually, he simmered down along about this part of the argument. "Maybe it's a good thing the frontier is gone. Now men can stop rushin' around and take a look at thimselves and stand still long enough to see that grass is green, th' stars are still in the sky. I've always had the feelin' there'd come a time when the world would get a bellyful of sufferin' and decide that it's easier to live peaceful-like than to be kickin' the other fellah's brains out."

Uncle Mike would lean his dark head to one side, an amused glint in his eyes.

"Civilization's about reached a peak, lad," Father would state flatly. "Why, I'm convinced they can't ever fight another war again. How d'ye like that?"

"Well now, is that so? And what's all the blather a'goin' on over there between the Turks and thim Italians this very minute?"

"A mere skirmish," Father declared. "The Big Powers know they can't afford to start a major war." He shook a horny finger under Uncle Mike's nose. "There ain't an army today that could stand up to a battery of these new Gatling guns. And cannon! They have sixteen-inch bores now on those naval guns . . . why, they'd wipe a whole town right off the map!"

"Maybe th' other fellahs will have sixteen-inchers, too," Uncle Mike would say.

"And now that man has taken wings, d'ye know they can dump high explosives over the sides of those airyplanes? I tell ye, man has outdid himself!"

Uncle Mike laughed. "Maybe when I strike it rich I better send for the whole family so's you'll be safe from them airyplanes and the sixteen-inchers, eh?!"

"Now none of your wise remarks!" Father roared. "I'm still your older brother and I want the respect of attention. I'm trying to tell ye it's time we all settled down and stopped daydreaming!"

Being nine at the time I took no part in these family discussions (if such they could be called, for at times they verged on mayhem), but I had definite feelings on the subject myself. It was my conviction that there never lived a man as adventurous, as glamorous, as daring as my Uncle Mike. And I knew that at the tender age of sixteen he had rushed off to enlist when the Spanish American War came along in 1898 (even then my father tried to stop him) and I knew Uncle Mike had been a real Rough Rider and had gloriously stormed San Juan Hill under Teddy Roosevelt. He never talked about his heroic deeds within earshot of my parents. I put this down to a masculine modesty befitting a man of his noble stature. Often, however, I would get him aside, perhaps up in my bedroom, or if the weather was warm, out in the backyard, and he would tell me once again how he stormed San Juan.

"Thim Spaniards," he'd say in a husky conspiratorial whisper, "were the very divils! Why lad, the shot flew around me like hail in a spring storm! And our boys were falling stricken mortal by the droves!" He'd always pause at that juncture and in remembrance of his dead buddies, a sad expression would cross his face. *"And old Teddy himself was right behind me, lad!"*

One night when I came into the house I heard Father and my uncle in one of their interminable arguments and I heard Father say: "Mark my words, Mike, you'll end up the same way in Alaska as ye did whin ye enlisted in Ninety-eight and spend th' whole damn war in a barracks hospital in Tampa recoverin' from the measles!"

And I heard my uncle say angrily: "Now Sandy, d'ye want to disenchant the boy?"

I didn't know what *disenchant* meant, nor could I understand what my father was driving at. All I knew for sure was that I worshipped Uncle Mike—he had heroically stormed San Juan Hill and he was so far up in front of the charging cavalrymen that even old Teddy himself was behind him.

While my father marshalled his powers of logic and tried to dissuade Uncle Mike—to no avail—my uncle had gone to the extent of incorporating himself for the big venture of his life. He held the controlling share of the Mullen Company to which he had contributed fifteen hundred dollars of his savings, my Uncle Aloysius putting up the balance of five hundred. Father remained adamant in his refusal to sanction this generous endeavor to make the Mullen clan rich; no amount of cajoling by my mother or sales talks by Uncle Mike could wheedle one red cent from his hard-earned savings.

"I spent years breaking me damned back a'buildin' locomotives for Sam Vulclain and what little pittance I've put aside will not be used to encourage a wild goose chase huntin' gold in Alaska." (Old Sam Vulclain, head of the great Baldwin locomotive works had once, years back, come through the foundry, slapped Father on the back and proclaimed loudly that he was the best moulder in the trade. Ever after that historic incident Father would declare when the slimmest opportunity presented itself that he built engines not for the Baldwin Locomotive Company, but for Sam Vulclain.)

So often did I hear the heated arguments between Father and Uncle Mike that I knew them by heart.

"I'll not be financin' any scatterbrained idjit to git himself frozen stiff up to-hell-and-gone in the Yukon!"

"Ah, be reasonable, Sandy. Now wouldn't it be better that I marry Bess whin I'm able to buy her sables and one o' thim expensive Pierce Arrows? Or do ye think it fittin' she marry a strong back with a weak mind that wrassles kegs o' beer fer a livlihood?"

"I'm buyin' a house with a little garden someday," Father would declare. "Annie and th' lads will have it whin I depart from this vale of ingratitude!"

Once when the air was blue with smoke and conflict my Aunt Bess had her say. "Listen to the pair of them! Nobody's asked *me* to wed...nor have I ever said I would!" She walked angrily into the dining room and returned with our Parcheesi set. "Come on, loser does the dishes," she challenged me.

We began the game while Father and Uncle Mike sparred and fought and tried to find a chink in the other's defenses. Finally, my Aunt Bess blurted out, "I'd like to get a word in edgeways to say I've been doing a lot of thinking...." Uncle Mike grinned at her expectantly. Pretty Bess hadn't spoken to him much of late.

"*This* is what I've been thinking! You, Mike Mullen, go off with your dogsled and pick and shovel. But don't be surprised to find that two can play the same game!"

Mother was sewing new window curtains on the Singer. "Now what in the world do you mean by that?" she said.

"Well," Bess said, "I'm beginning to believe there's a lot to what these Suffragettes say ... about women standing up for their rights!"

"Well, I *never!*" Mother gasped.

"Now let th' lass talk!" Father insisted.

Bess rose and almost upset the Parcheesi game. "I haven't begun ... if that shocks certain parties whom I could spit on from here without moving!"

"Now listen to herself!" Uncle Mike declared, "jist listen to the talk of the girl!"

She leaned across the table and Uncle Mike drew back.

"What I'm getting at is this ... don't be surprised if I turn up in Alaska myself ... wearing a red gown ... and singing my head off!"

Into the silence that followed, she added, "And it's a good voice I have ... as certain parties are well aware!"

"You're still underage," Mother said firmly, "and you'll be going nowhere without my consent."

Uncle Mike was a bright pink. "I never took me hand to a woman in me life, but b'jesus I've had enough o' this gab!"

"Oh, have you now?" Pretty Bess challenged. "I'm *past* eighteen and I think I'm winsome enough to get a job up there as a chanteuse!"

"*Chanteuse* she calls it!" my uncle roared.

"I've been readin'," Father said casually, "where those . . . ah . . . entertainin' ladies up in Nome and Dawson City got thimselves as much as a hundred ounces o' gold of an evening."

Mother turned on him. "You're as brazen as she is to use such language! That's what comes from reading that man Darwin! But perhaps he's right! Certain parties present *do* sound like second cousin to the apes!"

Father drew himself up; he inhaled deeply and his nostrils quivered. All this, as everyone knew, was his usual prelude to a profound quote:

> "The racer and hack may be traced
>   To one horse
> So men were developed from monkeys
>   Of course
> Which nobody can deny."

He paused: "Lord Charles Neaves!"

"Well, *I'm* denying it, and I don't know the man!" Thus deftly disposing of Father, Mother turned her wrath on her young sister who stood straight as a ramrod, looking sidewise down her nose at Uncle Mike.

"And you, my own blood!" Mother said. "Threatening to go off when the whim pleases you! I know what it is! It's that salacious novel that's done this!"

"Wicked, no doubt?" Father was bland now.

Mother ignored him, appealing to my uncle. "It's the one advertised in the papers. *The Dangerous Age.* Her Nibs had it with her when she came down last week. It's about a woman"—she spoke with indignation—"a woman who di-

vorces her husband and takes a trip around the world *all by
herself!*"

"And how d'ye know so much about it?" Father had
touched a vulnerable spot. He saw Mother blush and turned
to Uncle Mike. "I'm not so sure but what we might have to
reverse our opinions on the fair sex ... those ladies, up there
now ... those singers up in Alaska ... there's *real* miners
for ye!"

Uncle Mike jumped to his feet. "What this girl's hintin' is
shameful!" He walked angrily into the dining room.

"What do you mean ... hinting at what?" Mother called
after him.

He stuck his head around the archway. "She ain't talkin'
about singin' at all, the wanton! Those women she's referrin'
to are *women of ill repute, b'God!*" His underlip protruded.
"A red gown is it? The saints preserve us!"

Mother was truly stunned when the full meaning of Bess'
tirade dawned on her. My aunt calmly smoothed her hair.
"All I can say is I've given certain parties fair warning!" She
sashayed out of the room and went into the parlor, where
she began to play the piano and hum softly while I stretched
on the floor near her and read the funnies. Happy Hooligan
and Little Nemo. I also wondered what all the fuss was about.
What a family!

Well, tomorrow was another day.

CHAPTER III

Oh You Silv'ry Bells Jingle Bells

*Oh, there's snow on the ground all
    around dear,
And bells on the sleigh's merry
    sound dear,
Are calling my love,
Don't you want to take a sleigh
    ride, my turtle dove....*

DURING THE NIGHT it snowed. When I woke, some sixth sense wild creatures and young boys have in common prompted me to go to the bedroom window, but even before raising the shade I knew what to expect. The outer windowsill was a fluffy candy bar of white shredded coconut; the old two-story houses across the street had been magically transformed into gingerbreads with icing, and the narrow street below was a long, thin slice of vanilla cake. Since this was late December, and since I had weeks ago given up hope of a really good snow, I was tempted to emit a loud whoop of joy ... but Frank was still asleep in our mutual bed and my mother and father slumbered peacefully in the next room. So I did the next best thing: I opened the window and scooped up a hand-ful of snow. I licked it. I made a snowball, threw it at a cluster of bedraggled sparrows on the eaves of Nez Knowles' house across the way. My aim was bad, which was fortunate, because just then I remembered my pact. The night before I had made a deal with God: if he would make it snow, I would, for the next two weeks refrain from cussing, wash thoroughly every night before bedtime, run errands for Mother without the usual dawdling and (this a desperate concession) I'd do my homework.

The night before I had gone to bed fully convinced that my proffer of a celestial deal would be ignored, as it had been the summer before when I'd made Him a similar prop-osition. To wit: I would nevermore pester my mother with every stray mutt I found on the streets ... "Aw, it followed

32

me!" ... I would never, *never* again clip off the grocery list, I would somehow get Aunt Bess her feather hat ... and all in all, I would lead an exemplary life. All this in return for putting a Jehovian whammy on my mother: the Lord God would cause her to allow Uncle Mike to buy me a BB gun for my birthday. But my mother remained adamant: "I won't have the neighbors complain about broken windows, or ... perish the thought ... have somebody lose an eye from that murderous thing!"

So I didn't get the BB gun; instead, I got a weighty volume, *The Children's Book of Knowledge*, which I yearned for like two broken arms. My Uncle Mike felt as bad about it as I did and when he brought it down from Philadelphia on my birthday we went through the ceremony like two men facing a firing squad. My mother watched us with a proud smile while Uncle Mike thrust the book at me. "Well now, lad, it's a good head ye have on thim shoulders," he boomed. "Study this here book and someday you'll git to be President like Teddy Roosevelt himself!"

"Thanks, Uncle Mike," I mumbled. "I don't want to be President."

"Well, I *never* ..."

"Now, Annie," Uncle Mike said, "maybe the boy ain't got his heart set on it." He turned to me. "Run along and read about them grizzly bears. And comes the first snow we'll go off on a sleigh ride...."

The street had serene quiet as I looked out the window now on the specially concocted snowstorm brought about between God and myself. God alone knew how desperately I wanted this snow ... ever since Uncle Mike had repeated his promise: "If it snows, lad, snows *heavy* that is, I'll take you and yer friends for that sleigh ride."

Without giving him time to close his mouth, I nailed him. "You mean it, Uncle Mike? Cross your heart and hope to spit?"

"That I do, lad, that I do." He wagged a blunt finger. "Providin' of course, that it snows on my day off."

"How about a Saturday?"

"Now ye know I work on Saturday." (He drove a four-horse beer wagon in Philadelphia.)

We agreed on the first good snow on a Sunday or a holiday. I had been on a sleigh ride two years before, when I was seven, and it had been a glorious adventure. Many times since I'd pestered my father to repeat the performance, but there had been obstacles. "It costs hard-earned money to hire a rig for the day," he said. Or, "There's not enough snow, lad."

Father wasn't stingy. I knew that, but it broke my heart to see those stately sleighs standing idle in Old Man Armitage's big livery stable behind our house. Often I'd seen merry groups of men, women and children from other parts of the town come to Armitage's during heavy snowfalls and dash off happily in a sleigh. They were usually strangers, certainly not from our part of town, and when I raised the subject around the supper table Father became stern and tried to explain the facts of life to me. "*They* can afford it," he would say, his sharp blue eyes searching mine. "Three dollars means little to people like that. They're well-to-do folk." He would frown and run his powerful hands through his thin sandy hair. "And I only get one day a week to rest, and that's what I intend to do!"

Years of handling the heavy tools of his trade had turned this short, stocky man, who as a youth had come to this country from Ireland, into a callus-handed, muscular man who could wield a short-handled sledgehammer like a feather. I was proud of him. Never did a train run through the town that I didn't stop and watch with awe as the huge locomotive filled the heavens with its roar, and say to myself: "My Father built that!"

I knew that we certainly were not "well-to-do," a vague

term that meant simply you couldn't buy everything that struck your fancy—but we were not in need; in fact, we were much better off than most of the families that lived in our robust, noisy neighborhood. Many of the men on the street were industrial workers, or else employed in the smelly slaughterhouse a block over from our street.

We were happy, well fed, warmly and neatly clothed and we all loved each other. And, I believed, there was more fun in my house than anywhere in the world. . . .

There was no clock in the bedroom but I didn't need one to know that it was about seven o'clock that morning. Distant church bells rang. I heard Mother downstairs in the kitchen. I scooted into the bathroom to wash and slowly the whole house was permeated with the fragrant odors of Father's favorite Sunday breakfast: broiled salt mackerel, home-fried potatoes and rich black coffee. A few moments later Father banged on the bathroom door.

"Are ye going to be in there all day?"

I hurried out and back to my room, dressed, roused my brother, and when we got downstairs Father was at the table, his sandy hair neatly combed, a white shirt open at the throat and his black vest buttoned tightly. Frank and I stood before Mother as she glanced at our ears and hands, while additional odors came from the great old coal stove: our breakfast—thick-battered pancakes and chunky Pennsylvania Dutch sausage.

During breakfast I frequently glanced out the kitchen window. A good snow was fine, but anything that bordered on a storm or a blizzard would rule out a sleigh ride. I frowned and wondered if perhaps God wasn't overdoing it a bit. Occasionally a lazy gust of wind elbowed the window and I heard the soft *shhh-plop* of snow sliding off the slanted tin roof. Too much snow would mean roads might become impassable. Furthermore, Old Man Armitage was peculiar, he refused to rent beasts if the weather was too bad.

Mother noticed my worried expression. "What's wrong? You've only eaten six pancakes!"

"He's anxious for Mike to come." My father's ability to read my mind annoyed me. He got up and walked to the window. I watched and hardly dared to breathe. He came back and sat down while Mother placed another mackerel on his plate. "Kind o' heavy, that snow," he said quietly.

"Aw, pop! It ain't more than a couple inches."

"We'll see, lad," Father said. "We'll see."

I never understood how Frank could be so unperturbed. He busied himself shoveling down pancakes and sausages that swam in a plateful of molasses. When food was around, the end of the world could be at hand, but Frank would eat first —everything in sight if permitted. Father used to say proudly of his chubby rosy-cheeked son: "The young one can eat his weight in grub inside any twenty-four hours, if his mother would only let him!"

While I worried about the extent of the snowfall, I began to think I had been double-crossed by Heavenly Headquarters and was on the verge of directing dire threats upward. There could be too much of a good thing! Had I been over-generous on my side of the bargain, and as a result was getting too much in return?

There was only one thing to do. I had, at nine, a bound-less faith in the Almighty; somewhere up there, immeasurable distances beyond the stars, sat God, bewhiskered, gigantic, in turn both loving and cantankerous. He was unpredictable, as peculiar in manner as the adults around me. You simply never knew what to expect.

I went up to the bedroom, closed the door and got down on my knees. The night before I had promised much in the personal hygiene department, in addition to swearing off dawdling and to perform my homework punctually. Ap-parently I had gone overboard in promises. So I closed my eyes: *I guess I made a mistake, God. I take back what I said about doing my homework.*

I rose and went to the window. As I watched, the thick curtain of flakes slowly thinned, the wind gave forth a few choked, dying gasps . . . and the sun came out. I breathed a knowing sigh of relief and went downstairs, convinced more than ever that a guy had to be very careful. You could overdo the thing. . . .

When I returned, there was a loud knock at the back door, My father frowned. Using those silent signals I had come to know instinctively, Mother motioned me to see who it was. It was my gang: Moisha and Davey Katz and Hank Webster and Nez Knowles. They had watched the weather as avidly as I had, for they, too, were invited. I had extracted sundry small favors from them on the strength of the invitation, tribute in the form of juicy kreplas—cheese-filled, dough-covered triangles Moisha snitched from his mother's cooking pot; a chunk of Congress cake Nez filched from the bake oven and a powerful slingshot from Hank which I had long coveted.

The four of my gang tumbled in like a small unformed lump of humanity, cheeks aflame and bundled to the eyebrows. Mother frowned. She wanted Father to have at least a minimum of peace and quiet on Sundays; until Uncle Mike arrived and took us off, peace and quiet would be merely a desperate desire and Mother knew it. Up until that moment the kitchen was what might be called normal; but with the loud entrance of my gang, it was minor pandemonium. They babbled happily, bumped into each other, and Davey, tiny and squat-structured, fell to the floor with Nez Knowles. The latter was called Nez because the most prominent feature of his face was a long, pointed nose. Hank attempted clumsily to help Davey to his feet, but Davey growled and took a short poke at him.

"Now behave yourselves!" Mother warned.

"B'god," Father muttered, "I'm glad we never had triplets!"

Hank nobly overlooked Davey's offer to do battle. Hank was the tallest and huskiest of the gang. His father was a trolley conductor on the Pennsylvania Rapid Transit that ran rocking and swaying every hour from our town up to the big city of Philadelphia. My friend Hank rode free on his father's trolley, but he could never get his old man to bring us in on the deal.

Hank, Nez, Moisha and I were the elders of the gang. We seniors would engage in fisticuffs among ourselves on occasion, but there was an unwritten law that barred fighting with the younger set. You didn't do battle with your inferiors; you simply socked them when they got out of line.

Moisha glared at me with a wild stare, and though he always stuttered badly I knew what he meant to say:

"It sn ... sn ... sn ..."

"I *know* it snowed," I said.

Hank declared: "Mother said I gotta be back by supper."

"If you ginks don't be quiet, Uncle Mike won't take any of us," I said. This had an immediate sobering effect. As did Mother's order to "take off your boots." There was a flurry, and in a flash four pairs of rubber boots were in a pile on the floor.

The quartet were no sooner seated on the floor around the coal stove when there was another knock on the back door. "What now?" Father sighed. "Ye didn't invite any other lads along?"

"No, pop. Just us."

A draft of wind blew in and I heard Mother say, "Goodness, Mrs. Katz, this is a pleasure. ..."

I couldn't understand why it was a pleasure, nor apparently could Moisha and Davey, who eyed their mother suspiciously. It was known among our set that of all the adults in the

world, mothers were the very hardest to anticipate—they
could, for example, shatter the fondest ambitions by a mere
elevation of the eyebrows.

Mrs. Katz wore a black, knitted wool shawl around her
thin shoulders. As a matter of fact, I hardly recall seeing her
without it, summer or winter. She was a small, pretty
woman who spoke English with difficulty since the Katzes
had come to this country only three years earlier. In her
hands she held a plate covered with a white cloth. Immigrants
like the Katzes, desperate newcomers to these shores in those
days, of necessity measured almost everything in terms of
food. They had known hunger, too much of it. You couldn't
put your foot into the house next door without Mrs. Katz
going to the stove or the cupboard, and a moment later there
would be bread or cake or tea on the table. The most constant word of command was "essen!" ... eat! Since their
arrival in this country, the family had had sufficient food,
but even back in the old country, no matter how destitute,
how hungry the elder Katzes had been, I'm sure their re-
sponse to guests had been the same—an ingrained dignity
and kindness that was summed up in the word: "essen!"

Mrs. Katz now put the offerings—a fresh-baked apple
strudel—on our table and smiled. Frank, still engrossed in the
remainder of the pancakes, gazed at the plate and reached a
pudgy hand toward it and Mother slapped the hand without
halting her conversation with Mrs. Katz.

"Oh, you shouldn't, Mrs. Katz ..."

"For the *kinder* ... so excited they are for the snow ride."

Moisha looked at me proudly. Davey glowered at his
mother and muttered that he'd have his brains bashed out if
he tried to grab a piece of strudel in *his* house. "For everybody else, she gives free!" he whispered. Davey was a cynic.

Our neighbor patted Frank on his head, apologized for her
intrusion, and departed. Next there was a clatter of feet in
the front of the house and Uncle Mike and Pretty Bess came

into the warm kitchen. As I've mentioned, tender-aged though I was, I was nonetheless madly in love with my young aunt and when I deigned to notice any of the females at school, I invariably picked a smaller model of her, with shiny black hair, a cream-white complexion and enormous black-lashed violet-blue eyes like Pretty Bess. Occasionally I would condescendingly look with favor on a similarly endowed woman with big brown eyes and the same kind of skin and hair—like my mother—but mostly they had to conform more closely to the image of Pretty Bess.

This morning, though, my attention was riveted on my Uncle Mike. I was thrilled. Uncle Mike was garbed in a new, enormous Arctic beaver hat with earflaps; he wore an awesomely proportioned sheeplined mackinaw, and he was shod in fur-lined leather boots that reached to his hips. His big hands were covered with fur gloves, each the size of a half-grown raccoon.

I heard Father snort but I ignored him. Uncle Mike struck a dramatic pose and in a voice that rattled the breakfast dishes asked, "Well now, how do ye good people like the git-up?"

"Jesus, Mary and Joseph!" Mother gasped and laughed.

" 'Tis the ghost of Explorer Scott himself!" Father shook his head and poured another cup of coffee.

"Now ye won't be gittin' me in any arguments this day, Sandy!" Uncle Mike turned from Father and embraced Mother. "Look at that snow! It's God's day outside and sure the Divil himself couldn't inveigle me into a scrap." Solemnly, Pretty Bess kissed Frank and hugged me.

"When are we going?" I wanted to know.

The gang was standing now, as eager to get off as I was. Uncle Mike took off his beaver, gloves and mackinaw. "It's off we go as soon's I have a cup o' coffee," he said.

"Me, too." Pretty Bess sat down next to Uncle Mike and hummed softly under her breath.

"Sing it out, girl," Father urged. He loved her rich, mellow voice. "Sing it out!"

"You don't have to coax Her Nibs," Mother said.

"Now, Annie, leave the girl alone," Father said. "The world can do with a bit o' song!"

"Well, she'd do better to spend some of that money she fritters away on silly sheet music and take voice lessons," Mother replied. She never quite approved of Pretty Bess' means of livelihood.

"It's just as dignified as standing at a dry-goods counter and have nasty women treat you like dirt!" Bess tossed her head.

Mother had been a salesgirl in Strawbridge's Department Store in Philadelphia before she married my father. "I didn't have to *sing* for them!" she said.

"Now girls, stop that nonesense!" Father complained. "Can't we have a little peace on the Sabbath?"

"Sure, she sings like a nightingale," Uncle Mike said.

Mother glared at him.

Frank, finally finished with his pancakes, slid one pudgy hand toward the apple strudel until Mother spun and snatched it out of harm's way. I could feel my legs getting numb with anticipation, my eyes glued on Uncle Mike's coffee cup.... It was, I swear, the longest cup of coffee in the world.

Father, meanwhile, leaned back and lit his pipe. "I see you're really goin' through with it." He stared pointedly at Mike's getup.

"That I am. *That I am!*"

"Now, Sandy," Mother warned, "let Mike alone."

"Let him alone, woman! Somebody ought to take him out and knock some sense in his thick head.... I'm only doin' me duty."

"Duty, he says . . ." Mike began.

"A word of which you have no knowledge," Father said.

Mike leaned forward, his blue eyes narrowed and his chin thrust out. "There's still barrels o' gold up there in thim streams and, by God, I'm goin' to lay hands on it!"

"Let the lad get it out of his system, Sandy." Mother touched Father gently on the arm. "If he doesn't, he'll never make a fit husband for her."

"Loony as a leprechaun," Father said, "and me own kin!"

The familiar argument was on again; I tried to head it off, knowing it might go on for hours, by searching under the stove to pull Albert's tail. Albert, our cat, could be relied on to respond, which he did now. Nobody, however, paid the slightest attention.

"It's almost ten o'clock," I said in a loud voice.

Davey and Nez squirmed with impatience, any minute now Old Man Armitage would give away his last nag and the dream of snowy adventure would be over before it began. Uncle Mike lit a cheroot and jabbed it angrily at my father, his deep voice crackling with excitement. "They're gone from the Klondike now, the fools've all gone or died with their boots on . . . but there's bound to be lots of gold still up there. And Missus Mullen's boy Michael is goin' up and get what's left in the ground!" He paused and his eyes glazed with the wonder of it. "Why, man, there's enough left to make us all rich as Christmas!"

"Croesus!" Pretty Bess glared at my uncle.

Father leaned his muscular body halfway across the kitchen table, his face flushed slightly with the heat of the stove and the argument. "Can't ye git it through that thick skull that the only sensible thing for a grown man to do is stop seein' rainbows everywhere and look down to his feet and think about strikin' roots?"

"It's Klondike ground I'll be strikin' into! You're ten years older than me, Sandy, and ye have a family—"

"So I'm an old man now, am I?"

"Now, Sandy, I didn't say that...."

"Well, let me tell you, bucko, in these ten years I've taken on a century of wisdom ... somethin' I can't rightfully accuse ye of!"

"Hear the man talk!"

"I went through the Panic only five years back. I had a wife and two children to feed when hunger swept the land...." My father gazed at his two clenched fists. "... and when there was naught a bit of work for a man to lay his hands to!" He raised his voice as he remembered the hard times when the bottom fell out of the nation. This was a favorite topic. "I swore then that never agin would anything sneak up behind me and threaten my loved ones." He leaned back, breathing hard. "Things are better now, there's work for an honest man; there's good girls waitin' to marry and wee ones waitin' to be born. Any man who skitters his years away chasin' fools' gold over yonder hills instead of diggin' his toes in and savin' what he can is an idjit, a plain damned *idjit*."

"You won't be so free and easy criticizin' when I come back with a barrel o' gold so heavy it'll take a six-horse team to pull it!" Mike shouted.

The ponderance of such wealth was too much for Frank. The small hand that reached—almost, not quite—the top of the ledge that sheltered the strudel, paused, groped, and came down with a shattered plate. I yelled, "How about the sleigh ride? How about the ride ..."

That broke it. Uncle Mike, red in the face from the verbal clash with Father, shrugged into his mackinaw, jammed on his great beaver. He turned to Pretty Bess. "Now I'm askin' ye once more ... will ye come on the sleigh ride with us?"

"I'll only put a foot outside this house today!" she said, "to go to ten o'clock Mass with sis!"

"Ah, 'tis a stubborn woman ye are!"

"And I may be here when you get back... and maybe I won't!"

"So the two of them have been at it again." Mother turned to Bess. "Don't be a silly girl. The ride will do you good."

"I'm thinkin' maybe the lass has more sense than any of us...." Father grinned. "This is the kind o' day civilized people stick close to the hearth!"

"Now b'jesus, I've heard enough!" Uncle Mike bellowed. "Come along, lads."

We lost no time in getting into our coats and shoved off with Uncle Mike. I loved Pretty Bess, but I'd dreamed of this venture as strictly a masculine affair. Women, to my mind, were fine... in their place. Not many hours later I was to regret this feeling. I would have welcomed the presence of Pretty Bess, my mother, any resourceful female....

Old Man Armitage rented Uncle Mike a three-seater, and for an extra twenty cents he threw in two great horse blankets. Our steed was a graceful, powerful mare. And so, harnessed and hitched, we were off in a flurry of bells and shouts.

We headed directly out of town and traveled at a fine clip on roads of crisp, still-white snow, blemished only occasionally by the manure of other passing horses. Once we stood upright in the sleigh and hooted at a man and woman who stood forlornly beside their stalled automobile, which looked for all the world like the name it bore then in 1912—a horseless carriage.

Uncle Mike drove superbly. In my mind's eye, his big bulk was lashing a team of ferocious huskies and the winter wind became the howl of a pursuing wolf pack. My gang, too, was awed by my uncle. His deep, resonant voice rose above the wind and the bells—he must have mentally swooped to Alaska too, for suddenly he began to bellow at our horse: "Mush, damn ye... mush!"

He sang and waved the reins and once he let me hold them. The others wanted a turn but I glared them down. He was *my* uncle. I felt a twinge of pity for Frank, who implored me with a look to let him try it, but Frank was too young. Uncle Mike divined my thoughts and turned kindly toward my brother. "I'll let ye drive whin I get back from the gold-fields, lad! I'll be buyin' yet the fanciest rig on the market!" He turned and included the whole gang. "Sure, when I come back I'll get ermine blankets to cover the skinny lot o' ye!"

An hour later we were a good many miles out of town in a strange, sparsely populated farm country I had never before seen. To our right and left were endless white plains of snow that hid the furrows of the neatly kept farms; brown hay-stacks dotted the countryside and we could see red barns and gray-blue phalanxes of woods as backdrop. Uncle Mike sang and our eyes sparkled.

Then, abruptly, without warning, the sky darkened, and within a few minutes we were in the midst of a blinding snowstorm. I heard Uncle Mike mutter savagely to himself: "Bad Cess to it! I should of brung me compass along..." and with that extrasensory ability the very young often possess, I knew for certain he was worried. At my uncle's command, we threw the horse blanket over our heads. The bright joyous day had become black and menacing under our covering. We huddled together silently. I shivered. It was Davey who roused my ire by blurting openly what I feared inwardly.

"Gee... we'll get lost and freeze to death!"

"Heck, we *are* lost!" Hank mumbled.

A small voice in our midst said, "I'm hungry"—who else but Frank?

Our conversation was muffled under the blankets. "I'll beat your brains out," I warned. "Uncle Mike knows all about snowstorms. When he gets to Alaska he's going to drive a dog team in *real blizzards!*"

Once Uncle Mike leaned back, lifted our blankets and shouted above the rising wind: "It's only a flurry, lads. It'll pass!"

Davey Katz, the cynic, didn't believe it, and an hour later we were completely lost, our horse and sleigh staggering off the road into the huge drifts. Several times Uncle Mike got off the sleigh and tried to find a bit of higher land to get his bearings, but to no avail. We had to face it; we were lost. Now we felt the stabbing cold that sliced right through our blankets. Moisha was the first to blubber. I poked him, but when he was quiet, Hank began ... "I wanta go home ..."

"Shut up!" I was scared, really frightened. There flashed through my mind the vision of rows of stiff frozen cod I'd often seen in the neighborhood fish stores. I heard my voice squeak ... "Uncle Mike knows what he's doing! He's training for Alaska!"

Nez said with muffled disgust, "Yeah, sure!" then added his invariable, "T'hell with it, men!"

Looking back after all these years I'm certain Nez was a split personality because of environmental circumstance. His mother was a meek, ethereal Quaker who somehow, perhaps during a weak moment of the flesh, married a tough, whiskey-drinking blast-furnace tender. Whenever a strange kid appeared in the neighborhood, Nez always let the new kid sock him first; I suppose that was the maternal-Quaker side of Nez. But after the kid foolishly socked, Nez would proceed to deliver an enthusiastic walloping to the newcomer— that, I'm certain, was the paternal influence. My friend Nez used one stock phrase when any problem baffled him, to wit: "T'hell with it, men." It was his father's favorite expression.

Finally out of the deluge of whipping gale and snow there was a shout. Another sled had pulled beside us, and my Uncle Mike all but fell out of his seat in his anxiety to greet a fellow adult. I heard voices, and then Uncle Mike was back on the sleigh and we slowly followed the rig, which was now our guide. Not long after we were in the warm house of this Quaker farmer who had found us on his way back from Sunday service. His wife clucked over us and gave us hot milk, and I heard the tall Quaker say to Uncle Mike: "It was God's will that I found you, friend."

Then to our surprise, he got down on his knees right on the big kitchen floor. We watched the farmer's wife bow her head. Uncle Mike looked embarrassed. Then, also to our surprise, he was on his knees. Davey looked at me. "Guess we all gotta do it, huh?"

"S . . . sure!" Moisha said.

In a flash we were all on our knees, but my prayer—and I knew it secretly—was a little blasphemous. I felt I had been *really* double-crossed. . . .

There were no telephones in the countryside in those days; they were scarce in town too . . . only places of business and the well-to-do could afford the gadgets. There was no way our families could be informed. As the late afternoon became evening, Uncle Mike several times suggested starting back, but the quiet-spoken Quaker dissuaded him. "In His mercy, friend, He brought you to haven. Don't go against His wishes."

The storm continued full force. It would have been foolhardy to try to get back to town, even if the roads were passable . . . and they were not. So we spent the night bedded down on the kitchen floor, covered with huge patchwork quilts.

We rose at five. There was no snow falling, but the Quaker persuaded Uncle Mike to wait until daybreak. When the gray light finally appeared on the horizon and the man and wife were out in the barn at chores, Uncle Mike lined us up.

He was solemn. "Now listen, lads . . . yer folk will be a'worried stiff, understand?"

We all nodded. We understood.

"So now, I think it's best . . ." he winked " . . . I think it'll be best all around if we tell them that I kind of dragged the horse along through the storm and found this house—"

"What about the farmer finding us?" Hank asked.

Nez rarely spoke, but he was puzzled. "Yeah, if'n it hadn't been for the man we mighta froze!"

I turned fiercely on these ingrate fools. "You want they shouldn't let us ever go on a sleigh ride again?"

That did it. They agreed.

On the way back, only Uncle Mike was quiet. He kept the horse going at a fast pace, and in little more than an hour we pulled into our street. Doors flew open. Faces appeared at windows. My father burst out the front door in his shirt-sleeves and ran toward us; behind him was my mother and Pretty Bess. In the clear morning light they seemed to have aged. As we were being pulled from the sleigh, I saw Moisha and Davey's parents and Hank and Nez' mothers. People shouted, milled about, and out of that welter I saw the blue coat of a policeman who stood on the sidewalk—an annoyed expression on his cold, red face.

"It'll be good sense to get them youngsters in outa this cold!" he shouted.

Our house was jammed. Anxious mothers, men garbed for the day's work, kids ... it was bedlam. Pretty Bess flung her arms around Uncle Mike's wind-chafed neck; he patted her head and muttered, "Now, now lass ..."

I took my cue. I looked my father straight in the eye and said: "Uncle Mike saved us, pop. He got out and pulled the horse himself until we got to a farmhouse."

My father glared at his younger brother. "And I suppose ye'll be tellin' me he had to *carry* the nag on his back!"

"Oh, Sandy, they're all safe ... that's all that matters!" Mother said, hugging Frank.

The neighbors eventually went off, and Uncle Mike looked at his heavy gold watch. I had never seen him so subdued. "Well, it's off to Philly, or I'll be losin' me job."

"And it's that weak mind, such as it is, ye'll be losin' if ye still intend to take a crack at the Klondike!" My father threw his hands up, grabbed his overcoat and prepared to leave for work. "Lost in a little snow flurry right in his own back yard!"

He stormed out of the house and forgot, for once, to kiss Mother goodbye.

CHAPTER IV

Jimmy Valentine

Look out, look out for Jimmy Valentine
For he's a friend of mine,
A sentimental crook
with a touch that lingers
In his sandpaper fingers,
He can find the combination of your pocketbook...
Look out.... look out....

Look out for Jimmy Valentine....

CRIME DOES NOT PAY. I don't mean small embezzlements toward an ostrich-feathered hat. These were sacrificial for my aunt. I mean real crime. I began my experiment in shady dealing at a tender age and I've never since stolen, gypped, forged, misrepresented, connived, defaced, defrauded, swindled or knowingly fractured any federal statutes or local laws. My one early attempt to operate beyond the pale permanently soured me on ways that are evil.

As I've told you, there was a candy store in my neighborhood, and the smells that wafted from the place were soul-shattering ... enough to cause any nine-year-old to lose his grip. You might be walking home from school, careful not to step on a line on the sidewalk, thus outwitting Hard Luck ... or you might walk sidewise, just for a change of pace, and then you'd approach the candy store, its heavenly odor would ensnare you ... the delicious aroma of burnt-sugar drenched coconut mounds, shiny chocolate creams, glistening pink wafers, green or red clown hats with marshmallow bottoms and a luscious cordial inside, golden peanut brittle, brown white-dotted nonpareils, licorice straps ... and in the window, that great beautiful glass jar filled with edible jewels the colors of the rainbow.

This day, homeward bound from school, I saw my friend Hank Webster rooted in front of the candy store in a state of complete collapse. His freckled face was pressed against the pane, his red tongue hung out and his eyes were glazed. I got a whiff of the aroma permeating the immediate vicinity and felt myself going as well. I staggered over beside Hank and joined him in his trance until the sharp April winds and the cold plate-glass forced me to withdrew my nose.

I looked at Hank. "I got two cents," I said.

His nose still glued to the window, Hank felt around in his mackinaw pocket. "I got one," he said dreamily.

A tiny price sign on a cut-glass bowl of peanut brittle read: "8 Cts. Per Pd." I regretted my inattention to arithmetic in school, for I realized this represented a knotty problem in fractions. We had three cents. *Three goes into eight . . .* I gave up. Hank came out of his reverie and divined my thoughts.

"If'n that peanut brittle was nine cents a pound, we could git a third of a pound. Right?"

"He won't sell less'n half a pound," I said. "We need another penny." Desire made Einsteins of us both.

We fell silent again and cogitated upon ways of raising another cent. Then fate took a hand. The proprietor saw us and beckoned us to come in. He had hardly lowered his hand from the come-hither gesture when we were already standing before him, eager with anticipation. He stooped behind the counter and produced a large white box and placed it on the counter.

"I vant you boys to see dis," he smiled mysteriously. We were fascinated. He opened the box. Nested in pink and blue straw paper was a gigantic Easter egg, decorated with a thick white candy trimming and on top of which sat a yellow candy bunny. It was incredible! And we knew without being told that in the center of the immense chocolate egg there reposed a golden glob of pure maple sugar. We were speechless. The tempter let us feast our eyes for a moment, then put the cover back on the box. He produced two punchboards. We began to glimpse the light.

"You boys," he said smoothly, "can earn zomething between now and Easter. Yust sell these chances and I giff you fifty cents. . . ." He reached into the display case and took out a small half-pound chocolate egg—quite an anticlimax after the huge ten pound deal we had just slavered over— "either fifty cents . . . or this delizious reward."

"We'll take the egg!" Hank and I said together.

My pal held out his hand expectantly, but it became painfully apparent we hadn't yet learned the cruel code of the Business World: produce and you get paid—not before. We listened raptly as the proprietor briefed us. Each board had fifty girls' names, from Ann to Zelda. Each chance-taker punched a small red dot under a selected name and a tiny, tightly rolled paper popped out stating the price, from five to twenty cents. The guileless customer wrote his name and address on the back of the board beside the name he had selected. We were to collect seven dollars. On the upper left side of the board was a gold paper seal. Under it was the winning name. We departed from the candy store with an advance bonus, a half pound of peanut brittle for *three* cents and a couple of licorice shoestrings for good measure. Easter was ten days off and we estimated we had to sell five chances a day to make the grade. That we were being taken advantage of, considering the amount of legwork involved, never entered our minds. A healthy boy's appetite makes him a natural sucker for a big chocolate Easter egg. Furthermore, we were splendid examples of our time—the heyday of Free Enterprise—a now extinct era of American life.

My first customer, some hours later, was Father. He put his newspaper down and growled at my intrusion.

"Now what would I want with such a thing?"

"Well," I said, "maybe if you sorta win, I could sorta take it off your hands, pop."

He sighed and decided to select Mother's middle name, Loretta. The little tab he punched read nineteen cents and he paid off with bad grace. Next I approached Mother.

"I will not!" she said decisively. "All my life I've taken chances . . . church affairs, raffles and whatnot . . . never have

I won so much as a plugged nickle!" I started to give her a
razzle-dazzle sales talk but she looked me straight in the eye
and said "NO!" I departed. In the alley I came upon Moisha,
Nez, Davey and my little brother Frank.

"Whatya got?!" Davey demanded. I explained. It was
young Davey who thereupon launched me on my Criminal
Career.

"Whyn't we peek under the seal and see the winnin' name?
Then we can divvy the prize."

Moisha began to wave his hands, got red in the face as
though he were going to explode.

"That'd ... that'd ...."

"Yeah," I said sternly to Davey, "Moisha's right ... that'd
be cheatin'. . . .."

Davey glowered at Moisha but said no more. I started to
leave. "I gotta drum up customers."

Moisha held out six pennies and stared at the board.

"Nope," I said, "you might pick a twenny cents one." I
shoved my face against his. "You got twenny cents?"

"Let him!" Davey howled with glee. "Go ahead ... let
him!" Davey was a great one for getting other people into
trouble. But I wanted to get away and think. An insidious
thought tickled my mind. I left my colleagues jumping up
and down in some manner of argument and walked off.
There was, I recalled from what I'd heard Mother say, a
boardinghouse lady in our neighborhood who got into a peck
of trouble. This boardinghouse lady had an insatiable curiosity
—she used to steam open and read letters that came for her
charges. Nosey. I glanced at the gold seal and ran a grubby
finger over it. *Steam. Envelope flaps. Steam. Mucilage.* Under
the gold seal was the name of the winner. I closed my eyes,
swayed a bit. Holy cow! In my mind's eye that Easter egg
loomed enormously—it had doubled in size! I continued walking, oblivious to the clatter of wagons and street noises. I felt
the sweet caress of Temptation. My feet took over. I knew

where they led me. The Ice House. In the rear of the Ice House—and every kid in the neighborhood knew it—a fascinating pipe stuck out into the open air and emitted a constant billow of steam as an exhaust for the machinery inside. Often we had driven the night watchman batty by inserting a wooden plug into the pipe with a few whacks of a brick, standing aside while the pressure built ... and then WHAM!

My mission this evening was different. It was now dark, but there was moon enough for my purpose. The river air tingled with tiny needles. I shivered from the enormity of what I was about to do. The night was ghostly with anonymous peering eyes; somewhere a dog howled and I jumped. Momentarily I was numbed with indecision—would they find out and send me to jail? A few miles to the south, I knew, across the Delaware state line, was the whipping post they used for Wifebeaters and Drunkards. Would they tie me to that awful thing and whip me to bleeding shreds? I wavered. Until the mental image of the huge Easter egg intruded. It was bigger than ever, now the size of Mother's immense roasting pan—too much for mortal flesh to resist. I held the gold seal into the billow of steam, waited briefly until the mucilage melted. I withdrew the board, lifted the seal. It came up nicely. The name was Muriel. I replaced the seal. My heart pounded. I felt I'd come apart at the seams. From now on I'd be the most hunted criminal of all times. Police all over the world would engage in a full-blown manhunt for the slick crook who would mysteriously flit in and out of world capitals and rook punchboard operators out of Easter eggs, fountain pens, five-dollar gold pieces and other booty. I envisioned helmeted cops and plainclothesmen as they panted along behind bloodhounds as I, fast as the wind, flew over windswept fields and hurdled mountains, my arms laden with ill-gotten gains. I started homeward. I swaggered. They would place "Wanted" posters in the post offices. I'd often seen them—pictures of men who looked solemn and needed a shave. "WANTED!" But I would wear a disguise and they wouldn't know what I looked like. So, I thought grimly, they would have to put up *different* kinds of posters bearing the picture of a giant Easter egg, and beneath it would read: *Wanted: The Great Easter Egg Crook! If You See a Man Carrying a Egg Like This Call the Cops!* And I would be mean and harass the police. I'd be sarcastic and send them jelly beans through the mail with printed notes: "Beware . . . I Will Strike Again!" and the notes would be signed: "World's Champion Easter Egg Crook" or just simply "Jimmy Valentine, Jr." (The Willy Sutton of his time).

When I arrived home Mother asked me how many chances I'd sold. I looked at her with my best mysterious expression, shrugged and went upstairs. I heard Father's voice, a growl: "If the lad thinks he'll sell them all to me he's looney!"

"Wouldn't surprise me a bit." Mother laughed. I undressed, propped the punchboard on the chair, crawled into bed. That night I had a whammy of a nightmare. I was smothered in the maple sugar heart of a tremendous Easter egg struggling for air. Next I was being pursued by a pack of baying bloodhounds . . . all resembling Easter eggs with legs and yellow ears. I ran until I saw a big steam pipe and dived right into its blistering mouth. Drenched with perspiration I awakened, my head under the blanket. . . .

A few days later, right after supper, we had a surprise visit. Pretty Bess walked in, accompanied by a tall skinny man holding a gray bowler in his hand and wearing a dark suit with a heavy pinstripe. Mother, flustered, untied her apron and tried to smooth her pompadour.

"My heavens, Bess! You should let a body know . . ."

Bess took off her hat and introduced her gentleman friend. "Sis, this is Mr. Fortesque. Mr. Fortesque, meet my sister Anne."

Mother glared at Pretty Bess and managed a smile for the tall skinny man. "Pleased, I'm sure."

Although she tried to be polite, Mother, I saw, was both embarrassed and annoyed. More than once Father got in a jam by appearing at the house with some unexpected friend. Mother liked to be warned, she wanted to be what she called *presentable* when company came, and she rebelled at meeting strangers when she was garbed in housedress and apron, her usually immaculate hair even a little untidy.

"And this..." Aunt Bess said, hugging me, "this is my nephew."

Mr. Fortesque bowed to Mother and brushed me with a glance that made me feel like I wasn't there. I didn't like him at all. His patent-leather shoes were encased in gray suede spats and a tiny red bud reposed in the lapel of his coat.

"Hello, Mr. Fortesque," I said. "Some spats!"

"The latest," he said casually, "direct from Strawbridge's."

Just then father came in, and while Pretty Bess introduced him to the visitor, Mother excused herself for a few minutes vowing (with a hollow laugh) that she didn't intend to have Mr. Fortesque go away with the impression she was somebody's maid. She fled upstairs as Father produced a bottle of Irish whiskey.

"I hear y're in the singin' business," he addressed our guest.

Mr. Fortesque accepted a glass and bowed slightly in acknowledgment. "Somewhat, sir! You might say we provide the wherewithal." He smiled expansively and turned a look of admiration on Pretty Bess. "For them who're talented to do the singing."

My aunt flushed and smiled.

"Indeed?" Father said.

He poured himself an unusually large slug and I could see he had to make an effort to be the friendly host. Without question, Mr. Fortesque displayed all the earmarks of prosperity. His clothes smelled expensive, his nails were shiny, and I caught the glint of a diamond-chip ring on a finger. Well, all right, he was Big Business. I was in business too—punchboard business—and I began to think upon ways and means, at the earliest possible moment, of nailing the visitor to buy as many Easter egg chances as the market would bear. I went up to my room, picked up the punchboard, returned unobtrusively and stood off, clasping it within the clear visual range of Mr. Fortesque.

Father tried to force conversation, and I could tell from the strained look in his eyes that the role of perfect host was wearing thin. "Maybe ye'd rather have a bit o' tea instead of whiskey?" he asked.

Mr. Fortesque shook his head and smiled thinly. He emptied his glass in one gulp. I found myself intrigued by the size of his Adam's apple—I wondered if anyone had ever told him it was big enough to hang his gray bowler on. "Never touch the stuff."

Father cleared his throat. "Nice weather, eh?"

"Yep. Good track weather."

Father blinked. Mr. Fortesque smiled tolerantly. "Horses," he said.

"Oh." Father nodded. He'd never seen a horse race in his life.

There was a longer pause and Father glanced over Mr. Fortesque's head toward the doorway. Where was Mother? What the devil was taking her so long?

"Sad thing indeed . . . that *Titanic*, wasn't it now?"

"Yep, and I'd like to have a small part of what went down in her purser's safe!"

Father looked sharp at Mr. Fortesque. "I was thinking about those poor people."

Mr. Fortesque smiled and nodded.

Father coughed, then said grimly, "I see by the papers Teddy Roosevelt's Bull Moose Party's got President Taft kinda worried."

"Never read the papers," Mr. Fortesque said airily, "only *Variety*. That's my speed."

Mother reappeared and even to a son she looked beautiful. She had changed into a long blue skirt and ruffled shirtwaist, and she wore the lapel watch that glittered in the light of the kerosene lamp. The skinny man scrambled to his feet, smiled, and bowed from the waist. I began to sneer—this bow routine was annoying, and furthermore, Mr. Fortesque had absolutely ignored me and my punchboard; his infrequent glances in my direction were, I thought, fisheyed—just like the dead cod on display at Mr. Goff's store down near the wharf. He seemed to look right through me, and through the punchboard, which I held in various outrageous positions to attract his attention. Father, too, seemed oblivious to my presence. Only Aunt Bess squeezed my hand and pulled my ear.

When Mr. Fortesque told Mother she was charming, Mother flushed and said it was just an old rag really, and not at all new. Father grunted. Then Mother beckoned me to the kitchen, where she took a quarter from the old sugar bowl. "Go to Schiller's and get a quart of strawberry ice cream. We have company, so hurry back."

I took off like Barney Oldfield. Mr. Schiller refused to enter into a complicated deal with me when he filled the square quart container away above the top. "No," he said firmly, "I can't swap any merchandise for two chances on thet there punchboard. Now pay up!"

I paid and left.

When I got back, Father and Mother were sitting up straight and stiff on the horsehair sofa, Aunt Bess was near the window playing with the beads on her handbag—and Mr. Fortesque turned left and right on the revolving piano stool, his toe swinging easily along the carpet. They were all very polite, but only Mr. Fortesque seemed comfortable. The conversation had to do, it appeared, with the state of the world (this was Father's contribution); the nature of the song publishing business and its bright prospects (this from Mr.

Fortesque); the mental instability of young ladies, unmarried and under twenty-one, who yearn to travel across the country singing as a means of livelihood (that, naturally, Mother's offering). Pretty Bess maintained a strained smile and Mr. Fortesque, resistant to Mother's repeated attempts to get the talk down to brass tacks, smiled, nodded, crossed his knees showing his garters, and ran a smooth palm over his slick hair.

"Mr. Fortesque," Mother said finally, with firmness, "the girl here has mentioned working for your firm."

"There ain't nothing definite," Mr. Fortesque answered, smiling. "It's up to the boss, Mr. Franklin." He coughed and snapped his celluloid cuffs. "The idea's kind of new, sending song pluggers on the road. We've had a few pluggers working locally in the East, but I've been tryin' to sell Mr. Franklin on cross-country itineraries."

Mother seemed relieved. "Then it's still not definite ... it's up to your Mr. Franklin?"

"That's the general idea, ma'am." He smiled at Pretty Bess. Even his teeth flashed and I caught the odor of pomade. "But I think the boss will see the business aspect of it."

My aunt gazed pensively at Mr. Fortesque. Obviously, her fate depended on him. She colored and bit her lip.

Father saw the blush. He cleared his throat. "What might be your firm's name?"

Mr. Fortesque produced a business card and handed it to Father. "One of the biggest!"

"Jerome H. Remick Company," Father read aloud.

"Yes sir, right up there on top! Right along with Fisher and Von Tilzer!"

No one said anything. Father leaned back against the horsehair in defeat. Mother bit her lip. Finally my aunt spoke up. "It's a fine concern, Sandy. We sell their song sheets like hotcakes."

"*Do* you now?" Mother interjected.

"Yes, sis." Pretty Bess nodded toward Mr. Fortesque, "And

I'm going to sing for Mr. Franklin as soon as he comes down to Philly from New York."

Father frowned. "Then what, lass?"

"If Mr. Franklin likes my voice, I'll have the job."

"*Will* you now?" Mother said.

"Indeed?" Father said.

At this point Mother spied me holding the ice cream, rose and moved toward the kitchen. Mr. Fortesque also got up; he wondered if he might wash his hands. Mother told me to "Take the gentleman up and show him the bathroom." We went upstairs together. I stood at the bathroom entrance, my punchboard under my arm while Mr. Fortesque washed and dried and whistled a tune. This, I told myself, would be my only opportunity. I took a deep breath.

"Wouldja like some chances on a big Easter egg, sir?"

He turned toward me, his pale eyes narrowed. "It's not polite to hustle a guest, sonny. Beat it."

He rubbed the towel over his shiny nails and saw I was still there. Reaching into his pocket, he produced a dime. "Here. Now beat it!"

"Dontcha want a chance for the dime?"

"Go away, kid."

I went back down. My feelings about Mr. Fortesque were definite. I didn't understand him at all and what I didn't understand I didn't like. A gray bowler, resplendent on the cupboard, caught my sight as I returned to the living room. I laid the dime on the hat's brim and Mother called after me as I walked out:

"Don't you want any ice cream?"

"T'hell with it," I muttered.

"Do you or don't you?" she said. "What did you say?"

"Nothing. No," I said.

I managed to sell only once chance—that to Miss Louella West, a seamstress known to be a little absentminded—and when I came home Mr. Fortesque was, finally, ready to leave.

He stood with his hat in hand, elegant and stiff, and threw me a cold, disdainful glance. I managed a sneer, though I was careful that my parents didn't see it. At the mirror Pretty Bess primped back her hair; her lips were turned down and nobody seemed able to find anything to talk about. Finally my aunt pulled on her gloves and kissed me—but without her usual warm smile. Mr. Fortesque held out his hand to Mother.

"It was a pleasure, a gen-you-wine pleasure meeting you, Mrs. Mullen."

"I may say the same, Mr. Fortesque," Mother said. Her fingers, trapped in his clasp, looked as though they were made of soft rubber.

Father lit his pipe. Mr. Fortesque waited until Father blew out the match before he offered a hand. "Goodnight, Mr. Mullen," he said. "Nice evening."

"Goodbye," Father said.

He promptly sat down again and poured himself a shot of whiskey. Mother walked Aunt Bess and Mr. Fortesque to the door; when she returned, Father put down the glass with a bang and said: "I don't like the looks of him at all! Not at all!"

"He's tricky, that one," Mother agreed.

"He's a cheapskate, too!" I said loudly.

Mother turned, saw me and the punchboard, and said with annoyance, "Did you sell that man any chances?"

I decided to go around the truth as gracefully as possible. "No, Mom, I didn't."

She kissed me lightly on the forehead, then looked at Father again. "Sandy, we've got to do something."

"To be sure!"

"But what?" Mother said. "It's such a delicate matter— my own blood sister and all . . . and all the mix-up on Mike."

"You!" Father said to me. "Upstairs with ye!"

I was being mis-blamed again.

The next morning I arose feeling far less cocky. I glanced at the punchboard, and a terrible thought struck me. Wouldn't the candy store man know I'd peeped and rush around the neighborhood and tell everyone he'd unearthed an awful crook? The moment he saw my name beside Muriel, of *course* he'd get wise! My usual breakfast of oatmeal and tea finished, I trudged off to school, the punchboard under arm.

Later, in class, Miss Pennypacker added fuel to my inner burning conflict by assigning recitation for the next day on the topic: "Why Is Honesty the Best Policy?" Her sharp eyes searched the classroom for victims. I scrunched down, tried to evaporate. If she selected me, I swore I'd play hooky or break a leg. My own, if necessary. There was a long silence as she surveyed the class. She finally picked Hank and a coot named Chalky who greeted her selection with an explosive "Awww . . ." In the clear, I sat up.

The balance of the day I was not a model student by any means. Miss Pennypacker blasted me thrice for "daydreaming." She made me stay fifteen minutes after school to bone up on my spelling, and when she asked me, "What in the world has gotten into you?" I couldn't tell her I'd been busy trying to devise ways of obtaining the great Easter egg without putting *my* name down beside Muriel. In desperation I had toyed with the idea of putting Frank's name beside the winner, but I quickly discarded the thought, for my younger brother worshipped me, being a trusting cherub, and I couldn't involve him in the crime. And from the practical side, Frank with his staggering appetite for candy might insist on keeping the prize for himself. A ten-pound chocolate Easter egg would strain blood ties to the bursting point, I even thought, during classes, of approaching that coot Chalky and making a deal with him. But Chalky, I knew, was tricky. Hank swore he was a spy for our deadly enemies, the Potter Street Pugs.

The solution to my dilemma came after I finished my penance stint with Miss Pennypacker and she dismissed me. Why not put Father's signature beside the coveted Muriel? Who could suspect him? Who would dare question a man who could read right through a whole book and start right in on another? Brains! And everybody knew my old man was as on the level as Old Honest Abe—or, at least, I did—for the only time he ever really walloped me hard was the one time he caught me telling a lie. I took a deep breath and punched the tab under Muriel. Eleven cents. I didn't have it, but I would take care of it before I turned the board over to the candy store man. I scrawled my father's name on the book. *It was done.*

I ran into Hank. He looked harassed.

"Hi! How many you sell?" I asked.

"None. On'y forty-one to go. How you do."

"On'y sold three. My old man . . ."

Hank brightened and took off. I went the opposite direction, and the rest of the afternoon I pestered the life out of everybody I met, ducked in and out of stores badgering people, sold a few here and there. Old Man Armitage bought two chances when I cornered him outside his livery stable. He selected the names Violet and Daisy and explained these were the names of two race horses he owned years ago.

"Them nags never earned their feed," he chuckled as he punched the board, "and I bet they don't even *show* in this here Easter egg race." I thanked him and took off. By this time people in the neighborhood had begun to duck me— and probably Hank also—for I sold no more that evening. Eventually I went home, and so to bed. . . .

I dreamed of Monsters. All in the shape of Easter eggs. I looked up, and there towering over me like a menacing thunderhead, was a tremendous chocolate egg, slick and smooth, and before I could summon my benumbed limbs into action it leaned forward and fell, crushing me like a stepped-on ant.... The criminal way of life was slowly getting me down.

About a week later I was on the way out of the house—only ten more chances to sell—when Father gave me an appraising glance.

"Jist a minute, young man. What's wrong with ye?"

I didn't know anything was wrong with me, outside the fact that I was secretly a criminal. I looked at him, mustering all the innocence I could manage. "I'm all right," I said.

He felt my arms and legs, both wiry and on the lean side. "My God, ye're gettin' to be skin and bone! Do ye feel sick or anythin'?"

Mother came in from the kitchen, wiping her hands. "I've felt his head when he was asleep. He's had no fever," she told Father. All this was news to me. "I think it's that chance board thing that's doing it."

Father said, "Maybe we ought to get him to a doctor."

"He spends night and day selling those chances," Mother said. "He's overdoing the whole business."

Father took the punchboard, and my heart dropped. If he looked at the *back* of the board and saw his name in *my* inexpert handwriting, there would be a lot of explanations needed all around.

And then, even through my fear-wracked wits, came the perception that incredible Good Luck might just possibly be about to strike this miserable sinner as I heard my mother's gently reproving voice saying, "Now, Sandy, you mustn't, you really shouldn't..." and obviously hoping he would anyway....

And, schemer that I was, I calculated rapidly... what could be a better way to hide my criminal tracks than to have my father, as my mother was hinting he was about to do, buy the remaining ten chances himself? Boy! Who could question *his* right to want to win that big Easter egg or just help out his poor oppressed kid? I waited, my pulse beating against the roof of my mouth, while Father examined the board, slowly and thoughtfully. He looked up and his voice was stern:

"Listen, son. I'm goin' to take the rest of these chances, though the good Lord knows I can't afford it."

"Yes, sir," I said, fighting to control a show of relief.

"On one condition." He held up a finger.

"Yes *sir!*"

"On the condition that ye never again get mixed up in any more such nonsense! Agreed?" If Father had demanded it, right then I would have sworn the ultimate *cross my heart, hope to spit*, the most solemn oath resorted to by all nine-year-olds of my generation.

Father took the last chances and luckily they were all low priced, but it still cost him a little over a dollar, a large sum in those days when a good mechanic earned only ten dollars a week and a shop foreman about twenty. I went up to my room and counted my loot. I had, in the meanwhile, collected my own eleven cents; the mound of change came to seven dollars even. I sat for a while, gazing at the stupendous sum of money.

Now that I had the great Easter egg for my own—that is, as soon as the candy store man pulled the seal—I somehow didn't feel so elated. I imagined there would come a day, maybe in school, when a whole bunch of cops would crash into the schoolhouse, guns drawn, looking for me. I would make a spectacular leap out the second floor window to the overhead telephone wires outside, like those trapeze guys I'd seen in the circus, and I'd walk tightrope on the wires while the helplesss cops gazed up at me, stunned at my daring, and the whole student body would hang out the window and shout their amazement...and then I would deliberately plunge to the hard sidewalk below and die heroically, gasping my final words to my fellow men...that it doesn't pay to be a crook...and the cops would take off their hats in deep respect while Miss Pennypacker would regret many of the nasty things she had said about me.

I went back downstairs feeling very tragic and decided to go out and round up the gang. I climbed the high fence in our back alley and sent out a few treble hoots. No answer. Then I saw Old Man Armitage sitting on a bale of hay outside his livery stable. I felt like talking to somebody. I liked him, in fact we all admired Old Man Armitage because he had one of the best jobs in the world, next to firemen or locomotive engineers, and what he didn't know about horses wasn't worth knowing. I got down off the fence and went over to the old man, who was smoking one of his long, foul cigars. I knew he had a home somewhere, but most of the time he stayed right at the stable and slept on a cot in the small cubbyhole which he also used as an office. There were at least forty horses in the stalls every night; some were sleek specimens, carriage horses belonging to the well-to-do in town; mostly, though, they were massive-muscled beasts used to transport coal, ice, fish from the wharves and produce from the adjacent farmlands where Pennsylvania Dutch wore chin beards and dressed in odd, formal suits of black. A few of the horses were plain mangy nags, like Mr. Katz's Becky, that belonged to junk dealers and peddlers. Old Man Armitage loved them all. One of the reasons he did a profitable business the year round was because the horse-owners knew he gave more than their money's worth—he was obliged only to bed and feed horses; actually he doctored, curried, inspected their sore hooves and removed nails and glass, and above all . . . he talked to them.

The old man moved over on the bale of hay. "Sit down, sonny." He called all us kids "sonny."

The night air was chilly but dry. From behind us came stable odors of dusty grain, manure and ancient wood. He looked at me through the acrid smoke of his cigar. "Why ain't ye with the rest of the boys?"

"I don't know where they are," I said glumly.

"Umph. Looks like ye got somethin' on your chest."

He could read animal minds, so the story went, why couldn't he read mine? I looked up at the bright stars.

"What's wrong, sonny?"

"Nothing, I guess."

"Well, you had me worried there fer a spell. How's the chanceboard comin'?"

"I sold them all ... uh, Mr. Armitage, you know anything about crooks?"

He looked down at me, startled, and took the cigar out of his mouth. "Now that's sure a funny question, sonny." He thought a while. "Seems to me, after doin' a lot o' livin', that most crooks ain't where ye'd expect to find 'em." He glanced at me again. "Ye ain't gone and stole somethin'?"

I was stumped. I felt his old eyes studying me in the bright moonlight and I was sorry now I'd brought up the subject.

"Now look, sonny, if ye went and snitched some o' thim pickles agin ..." (he meant next door at the Pickle Works) "... why thet ain't anything to worry about. Seems to me they's just invitin' people to grab a pickle now and then, leavin' thim in the open in thet big vat. Jest invitin'."

I remained wordless.

"Or if ye grabbed maybe an apple over at the marketplace ... why sonny, there'd be somethin' wrong if you fellers didn't. Wouldn't be normal not to, seems to me."

"Yes sir," I said. There was another silent gap. Finally the old man said, "Was it money?" He was real serious now. I thought quickly. No, it wasn't money. I wouldn't dream of a thing like that. I was a more complicated kind of crook who had a failing for goldarned Easter eggs, big gobs of chocolate-covered Easter Eggs.

"No, sir, it ain't money," I finally answered him.

A horse whinnied and then repeated the cry louder. Old Man Armitage arose and carefully placed his cigar on a turned-over wooden tub. "That'd be th' Goff mare," he muttered. "Been workin' to th' heeves all night." He halted at the dark stable entrance and contemplated me. "Well, sonny, whatever ye did can't be so bad. Ye ain't lived long enough to soak up enough meanness to do somethin' real evil ... now git home with ye and t'bed."

I left feeling worse than ever. No one understood, not even a wise old man like Mr. Armitage. I wandered down the moon-drenched alley and thought of Miss Pennypacker and how often she had said, "Choose what you want to be early in life, then put your heart and soul in it ... great men shape their lives early." Boy! If she only knew! The World's Greatest Easter Egg Crook! Jimmy "Sweet-tooth" Valentine!

I went in the house, hung around the kitchen, brooding, and tried to entice Albert from beneath the stove. My father, in carpet slippers, was reading. That really upset me ... I mean, here I was, his own flesh and blood, probably slated for eternal flight from cops, and eventually to swing from the end of the hangman's rope—and here he was, totally oblivious of my desperate plight, engrossed in one of his old books. I decided to engage him in a bookish discussion.

"Hey, pop," I blurted, "you know anything about crooks?"

He dropped the book as though stunned. "Now, b'jesus, that does it!" He leaned close, narrowed his eyes. "Ye should have seven dollars on that blamed punchboard ... now, ye didn't *steal* any of it?" There was a pleading note in his voice.

"No, pop, cross my heart!"

He sighed with relief, picked up his book. "Well, now, what's this about crooks?"

"Aw, I only wanted to find out how a guy gets to be one."

"Hmm ... have ye been seein' these Pearl White movies agin ... or the train robber things?"

"Well ... sort of, pop." I was sorry I'd brought it up. I went to bed thoroughly disgusted. *Nobody* understood....

Then, once more Fate tagged me, this time with an iron

hand and hot claws. Mother came home the following day pleased as she could be, and especially nice to me. Naturally, I was highly suspicious. Nothing apparent to the naked eye called for this kindly, solicitous treatment. My last report card had simply indicated, to quote Father, I was "jist slightly on the safe side from bein' an idjit!" And nobody had actually *seen* me take a bath for weeks—they had only heard sounds of water splashing, this achieved by sitting on the toilet seat and kicking a foot in the water—no mean feat, I might add. So I was very suspicious.

"Father Ryan wants you right after supper." Mother smiled.

The floor collapsed beneath me.

"What's the lad done?" Father frowned.

"The Kelly boy came down with the mumps," Mother said. She patted my head. "His Nibs here is going to replace him in the choir—the Easter Mass."

I turned sickly green.

Two years before, I had been roped into the choir by Pretty Bess, after she boasted about my "beautiful soprano." I endured the stint for a while, along with thirty other angelic hellions, and was finally dropped when I carefully developed an earsplitting high C monotone that drove the choirmaster out of the church.

"I got a ragin' fever and a raw throat," I gasped. I staggered around, bumped into things, held my breath until I was bright red in the face, trying to look like 104.5.

"*Now* what's wrong with him?" Father said.

"Nothing at all," Mother said.

I howled.

"Right after supper," Mother said firmly, "*and be on time.*"

So I went. On the way I stopped every few feet and wailed as hard as possible. People stared and gave me a wide berth. This sustained howling, I'd learned from other kids, sometimes helped you develop a grating hoarseness and you'd be sent home. But when I got there I was, ironically, in fine voice. Apparently it had only helped tune me up.

The choirmaster beamed when I appeared. He smiled kindly when I declared I was subject to St. Vitus's dance and my hair was full of nits. He put me between two white-robed coots I didn't know and we began to give the Miserere a workout. As we swung into a high sustained note, I decided then and there I'd rather end in Purgatory than go through this for another week—knowing in my heart I was a Master Criminal and my very presence within these sacred walls an outright sacrilege. So I stomped hard on the toes of the boy on my right, hoping he'd turn stool pigeon. He bleeped in pain, recaptured the note, and without changing his rapt expression the slightest rammed his thumb deep into my ribs. I bleeped. The choirmaster frowned in our direction, but we continued without a hitch. I finally went home weighted down with Tragedy.

Several evenings later I concocted a fiendish plan to get thrown out of the choir, a plan inspired by an empty tin of Copenhagen Snuff abandoned on the sidewalk. I packed it with cotton, went under the Pickle Works fence and carefully tilted a generous splash of concentrated ammonia into the small container, quickly closing the lid. The odor was terrific. Then I went to practice. We were tuning in on *Gloria in Excelsis Deo* when I carefully reached into my robe, grabbed the snuff can and opened the top. I let it fall to the floor as I gazed rapturously to the nave, then skidded the can down the line with my foot. My eyes watered, I heard gasps, looked around cautiously. Now everybody was in tears. Father Ryan came in. His usually cheerful expression became instantly solemn. He whispered to the choirmaster, who was now terribly solemn himself. The singers nearest the can had to tilt their heads away back and really belt the notes in order to breathe. We finished. The kids wiped their eyes, glared suspiciously at each other. The choirmaster bowed his head and wiped *his* eyes. This intrigued me no end, because I knew he was too far out of range.

Father Ryan blinked. "Boys," he said, "that was the most touching performance I've ever witnessed. I've never seen such beautiful dedication. Bless you!" He walked off slowly.

The coot next to me muttered, "I'll bust ya wide open whin we git outside!"

"You and what regimint of th' marines?" I sneered.

I waited outside for my opponent. He turned up shortly. I had decided to achieve two black eyes, then tell my mother I was afraid to go back because a bigger boy had tried to kill me with a pole axe. We took off our jackets, slowly rolled up our sleeves. This was routine procedure. I swung. He swung. I missed. He didn't. All I achieved was a sore jaw. I returned home deep in gloom.

The next day after school Hank and I journeyed to the candy store clutching our money and the punchboards, my face swollen badly.

The proprietor seemed genuinely pleased as he counted our mounds of pennies, nickles and dimes. "Now," he said, rubbing his hands, "ve vill see who vins, eh?"

He reached over the counter and chucked Hank under the chin.

"Poot back de tongue or you lose it maybe!" Hank withdrew his tongue. The winning name on his board was Cecilia, and a woman several houses down from Hank's was the lucky winner. The candy store man produced a big white box containing a ten pound Easter egg. He took a pair of half-pound eggs out of the display case and placed them in smaller boxes for us.

"You giff de big one to de lady, eh?" He grinned at Hank, who nodded silently, dazed at the prospect. Then my turn came. The proprietor studied my punchboard. I swallowed

with apprehension. *This was it!* He pulled the gold seal.
Muriel. (Naturally.) He turned the board over to see who
won. He read Father's name aloud.

"Wow ... that's yer pop!" Hank blurted. "Yer *pop* ..."

"My Father took *twelve* chances," I yelled. Then for good
measure, I added, "And he's tough!"

The candy store man nodded calmly. "So, your fazzer, he
takes twelff, eh?" Then he glared at me. "And maybe he
writes his name two ways, eh?"

Hank's red tongue was hanging out again. I was sorely
tempted to give him a quick uppercut. But I stood firm.

"My father won!" I said flatly.

The candy man nodded. "He will get his prize, don't
vorry." He walked to the rear of the store, returned almost
immediately with a gorgeous huge Easter egg. I breathed a
loud sigh of relief. Shortly afterward we got to our street.
I quivered with excitement. I stopped along with Hank when
he delivered his great egg to the woman. She was elated and
cut two thick slices for us and we gobbled them on the spot.
Tender and heavenly. Then I rushed out and ran into the alley behind my house. Hank hurried home. Moisha, Nez,
Davey and Frank materialized from various nooks and cran-
nies and gave forth with piercing hoots when they saw the
big box under my arm. I was bursting with importance. I
put the box on the ground and opened it. There it sat in its
nest of colored straw paper—enormous, white-trimmed and
a yellow bunny on top. It was the creation of a candy-making
genius, the most delectable Easter egg since the Dawn of
Man. I raised my penknife with a flourish. "Wow ... here
goes!" I shouted. The gang stood transfixed. I began to cut
the egg. Something was wrong. I felt the blade. It was sharp. I
tried again. I began to sweat. The Easter egg was as hard as a
rock! Harder—like a chunk of iron. The gang got down on
their knees beside me, their mixed expressions between be-
wilderment and dawning horror. . . .

"Wazzamatter?" Davey squeaked, hurt in his voice.

Nez silently took the penknife out of my hand. I felt numb. Nez sawed and groaned. The only result was a thin scratch on the chocolate coating. My thoughts were gall. My jaw throbbed. Nez folded the knife, rose to his feet. He walked off angry at me and the whole world.

Davey said, "Maybe we kin soak it, huh?"

Frank said, "I'll get a hatchet."

Moisha had turned yellowish, "Maybe we...we... kin..."

I recalled then what Old Man Armitage said: "Most crooks ain't where you'd expect to find them...."

"Most crooks..." I began bitterly. But I saw my gang didn't even hear me. They all gazed blankly straight ahead, as though in a state of shock....

That night after the candy store man closed his place and went home, I scrawled one burning word on his door with a piece of red chalk. "CROOK."

And later that evening I got expelled from the choir without even meaning to. My mind was running riot with the injustices of Life, and as I sang, eyes closed in frustration, I somehow interpolated lyrics of my own while the massed voices around me provided a sonorous, magnificent background. I was so immersed in my litany of condemnation that I outlasted the choir and kept right on singing in a piercing soprano... *he's a crooo-oo-ook ... oh, yes, he's ... a dirty ... C-R-O-O-OK!*" I opened my eyes. It was so *quiet!* And *everybody* was staring at me....

Of course, when Mother heard, she consigned me to the Doghouse. The Sentence: Every Day After School For One Week. She also said I had disgraced her forever.

From that day to this, no Easter egg has ever touched this sinner's lips. Well, hardly ever....

CHAPTER V

Down Went McGinty

Sunday morning just at nine,
Dan McGinty dressed so fine
stood looking up at a high stone wall,
When his friend young Mat McCann says ...
I'll bet five dollars Dan
I can carry you to the top without a fall.

CHORUS:
Down went McGinty
to the bottom of the wall,
And tho' he won the five
He was more dead than alive,
Sure his ribs and nose and back was broke
From getting such a fall.

THE POTTER STREET PUGS OUTNUMBERED, outweighed and always outfought us, a perpetual frustration to the kids of my neighborhood and most especially to my immediate colleagues.

Fortunately the Pugs were geographically separated from our part of town and attended another school. If not for that fact I think seriously I might never have acquired any education whatever ... and when I say they *attended* another school I mean it in a figurative sense because the town's truant officer devoted at least ninety percent of his pursuits to the Pug area. There were about fifteen in the gang ... brawling, chunky sons of Polish and Irish immigrants, who traveled in a pack, and although they clobbered us on every encounter, in one respect at least we could feel morally superior. Our gang rarely stole. Nothing except pickles now and then or other prizes of similar minor magnitude. The Pugs however, in addition to being the terror of every group of kids in town, were picked up individually and collectively by annoyed cops for the theft of *real* things, such movable objects as were not nailed down or imbedded in concrete. Consequently when our gang got its lumps in an unexpected skirmish with the Pugs, we didn't feel too bad, for they were older and, in our eyes, beyond the pale of what we considered decency. For instance, the Pugs *smoked*. We also smoked on occasion but our indulgences were limited to corn silk ... if we really felt orgiastic, we might even go so far as Cubebs. The Pugs were known to be addicted to Sweet Caps and Piedmonts, the real thing, and we knew for a fact they were also addicted to

78

girls! This weakness puzzled Hank, Moisha, Nez and myself —we couldn't figure how they could be so tough and still display any real interest in the opposite sex. As for the smaller fry, my six-year-old brother simply didn't know there was any difference between boys and girls, and Davey Katz, while he was aware of the peculiar biological difference, had once expressed his feelings on the matter by stating with smug masculine superiority that boys had it all over girls because what girl could actually aim it over a four-foot fence.

Instincts of self-preservation should have prevented us from straying too far into Pug territory, but we were on one of our aimless barefooted treks this day, and soon found ourselves confronted by eight Pugs arrayed ominously on a railroad embankment. They had appeared without warning, like a pack of Mohawk marauders. Moisha sighted them first, went rigid, and pointed. As one, we halted. The Pugs began to descend toward us. From the bulges in their pockets we knew they were ready for battle. Stones. Carefully selected riverfront stones. Without a word we began to retreat, searching the ground for any throwable weapon of defense. Then Hank, glancing to our rear, swore . . . six more Pugs were advancing toward us from that direction! The embankment cut us off so we had only one escape route—a vast stretch of swamp. Stones began to fly. We floundered through the thick reeds as the missiles whizzed past, and Frank yipped and clapped a hand to his head.

All of us except my brother Frank had displayed at various times marks of our manhood; marks that varied from yellow-gray bruises, bluish head bumps, greenish-tinged black eyes and, not infrequently, minor gashes inflicted by the stones of these our mortal enemies. Frank, however, had never been eligible for that sort of Purple Heart. Now, at last, he was. I halted long enough to examine the damage. It wasn't much. A stone had bounced off the top of his head, but his hair was thick and had cushioned the blow. Nevertheless, he *was* bleeding. He was happy.

Covered with swamp mud, we managed to reach safe territory, marched Frank down the back alley, climbed over the fence adjacent to the livery stable and found Old Man Armitage. By this time Frank had managed to develop a swagger, much to Davey's disgust.

"You just wait till Old Man Armitage burns ya!" he warned Frank. "You'll see!"

Old Man Armitage often performed clandestine first-aid on various kids in the neighborhood. Our folks, of course, were never let in on this, and the old stableman never divulged our minor wounds. He probably felt that horses and young boys got more or less the same bumps in life. Anyhow, he treated both.

"What in tarnation now?" Old Man Armitage demanded, looking us over in an attempt to spot the wounded hero.

Silently, Nez pointed to Frank.

"Well, let me see it," he grumbled, "I ain't got all day!" We paid him little mind because we knew he always came through. He took Frank over to the horse trough and thrust his head deep into the fresh water. Frank attempted to protest but his head was under and all we heard were a few wet burbles. The old man examined the gash, clucked to himself, and produced the large white styptic pencil he used on horses and small fry. He pressed it into the wound; my brother whooped, splitting the air with a series of anguished bleats. But the job was done quickly on the small cut as though it were a branding iron. Old Man Armitage released Frank while Davey hooted: "I tole ya . . . see?"

Grounded after his brief flight of glory, Frank cast down his eyes and scratched one toe with the other foot. Old Man Armitage put away the medicine kit, then insisted we all dunk ourselves in the water trough. This was wise, we decided—we looked like something just dragged up from the bottom of the sea—and so we washed, put on our short pants and took off.

I well knew, though, that if Mother discovered Frank's badge of honor there would be hell to pay, with me picking up the tab. Therefore I carefully instructed my younger brother to keep his yap shut, never doubting for a moment that he would do just this, for Frank rarely spoke—his nose and his appetite being his favorite means of communication with the world around him.

However, this time I misjudged him. For once he had to assert himself. He had been wounded; he was no longer on probationary status with the gang. We were at supper before I noticed: Frank gazed at Father and actually ignored the huge slice of roast beef, mashed potatoes and gravy that Mother placed before him. He sat straight and square-shouldered, leaning forward a little, his innocent eyes shiny and his mouth squeezed tight as if he were ready to bust. Father caught his glance, frowned and stabbed a piece of bread. Frank sighed. Still wordless, eyes riveted on every gesture Father made, fixing him, compelling attention until Father—a little uncomfortably—swallowed the meat he was chewing and drank some water.

"Better call a doctor, the lad's sick."

"He looks all right to me." Mother leaned over and felt Frank's forehead. "My, you scared the daylights out of me! His head's cool as a cucumber."

"That grub's sittin' in front of him for a full ten minutes and he ain't even looked at it!" Father said in a worried tone.

"Sit up!" Mother said to me. "Won't you *ever* learn manners?"

"He's still not touchin' his grub," Father said. "I'm not insistin' he is, mind you, but when this one ignores his belly it gives a man cause for suspicion."

I slid down in my chair again and tried desperately to make myself as small as possible, for I knew what Frank intended to say and there was no way I could circumvent calamity at that moment. Mother turned her attention back to my brother. Her brows wrinkled.

"Do you have a pain, son?"

Frank shook his head—his baby mouth opened to speak—then he merely beamed at us all.

I tried frantically to locate his foot under the table to mash it into a bloody pulp. Anything, *anything* to divert him and prevent what I knew would come. But he was shorter than I and there was no foot to pulverize.

"At least it's not mortal," Father said when he saw Frank's grin. "Speak up lad, for I'll not relish this grand pie of your mother's with you sittin' there, your plate untouched."

His Big Moment at hand, Frank drew himself two inches higher in the chair and announced proudly: "I got wounded."

"You what, lad?" Father frowned.

"I've been reading him stories about the Silver War!" I interjected.

"Civil War!" Mother said.

"I got conked on the head," Frank persisted, his eyes never leaving Father's face.

I improvised, "This here story tells about the soldiers running out of ammunition and usin' their gun butts!"

Mother cocked one eye at me, closed the other, and I knew the day was lost. What would my chances be, I wondered, if I slid under the table, scooted out the other side and made a dash for it out the back screen door?

Meanwhile Mother got up, walked around my chair, placed her hands on Frank's head and addressed me in that funereal tone I knew so well. "What have you done to the child *this* time?"

As her fingers reached the gash, Frank winced. Father sat quietly, brooding, and I knew for certain that one of his slippered feet had begun to jiggle. This always signalled a kind of reverse reflex action prior to the delivery of a carefully calculated boot to my backside. Not a word was spoken in that tense moment; everyone was satisfied from past experience that whatever was wrong, I was definitely at the bottom of it. Guilty or not, I would be blamed. Mis-blamed.

Mother emitted a startled gasp, half shriek, half anger, as she parted Frank's Buster Brown and saw the tiny wound. I ducked. When I came out from under the table, Father was standing over me.

"The Potter Streeters did it!" I yelled.

Father secured a firm grip on my collar and during the next three minutes I was, in order, booted by Father (which I didn't really mind for it never really hurt), consigned to perdition by Mother, and upon command from both sent directly to my room.

Flopped across the bed I thought nostalgically of the *John Enny*, the magnificent six-master that sailed up the Delaware twice a year on a run from Hawaii to Philadelphia, its hold loaded with sugar. The inspiring visit of the *John Enny* brought crowds to the riverbanks and there was always something about the slow, stately progress of the old ship that filled me with envy. Condemned to my doghouse, I now decided to go to Philadelphia the next time the *John Enny* hit port and hide myself on board as a stowaway. At that moment the exotic, distant land of Hawaii didn't seem far enough removed from my parents, but it would have to do. You couldn't have everything.

I had begun to doze when Father came into the room with a plate of food. He looked at me, shook his head, and departed. At that moment I decided to starve myself to death. I envisioned myself slowly wasting away until I was a walking skeleton. Father and Mother would wring their hands and cry and beg me to eat and they would try to tempt me with great mounds of ice cream and enormous chocolate cakes . . . and . . . my mouth began to water. I made a dash for the plate of roast beef Father had put on the dresser.

Replete with nourishment and belching sadly, I cast around for other means that might drive my parents to a condition of pitiful remorse (I would, for instance, inflate a hundred colored balloons on the gas jet and soar miles above our house, refusing ever to come back to earth again...or I'd build a raft out of big kerosene drums, hoist a skull-and-crossbones flag and become a pirate) when my thoughts turned to the Potter Street Pugs. *They* were at the bottom of the whole affair! I seriously considered training to become the World's Champion Fleaweight, Junior Class. There was a boxers' camp a few miles from our town at Leiperville where some of the best fighters of the time worked out. I would train there mightily, day and night, turn myself (all seventy pounds of me) into a ruthless fighting machine. I'd burst into the Pug neighborhood and take them all on at once and when I was through there would be Pugs scattered all over the terrain, battered and bruised and forever fearful at the very thought of me. That was the only way to do it! Brains, force, all buttressed with resourcefulness, were needed. Genius, in fact, I decided, when I recalled that even my Uncle Mike, with *his* superb military mind, had been unable to help my gang outwit the Pugs. Lying forlorn on the bed, my stomach rumbling, I recalled that incident of the previous summer with bitterness....

Uncle Mike and I were out for a stroll and because he was with me, I dared venture into the area dominated by the Pugs. After all, even the Pugs wouldn't come near while Uncle Mike was around! So we sauntered along, the two of us, and we spoke of marvelous things that Sunday—he about how he had been a gandy dancer on the Santa Fe Railroad when he was mustered out of the army (after his superb charge up San Juan Hill, of course) and how he had routed

a tribe of Apaches singlehanded one night when the rail-
roaders' camp was attacked. His rich voice filled the warm
afternoon, and as we neared the Pugs section of town Uncle
Mike related how, with brilliant forethought, he had crawled
on his belly, Apache arrows and bullets droning around on
all sides, and had mounted one of the workhorses in a nearby
corral and turned loose a hundred more in a stampede that
trampled the Apaches into a panicked retreat. These and
many more marvelous things did he regale me with that day
as we walked and talked, man to man, the best of pals—and I
was convinced more than ever that a greater man never
moved on the face of this earth and I wondered why Uncle
Mike wasn't my father instead of the book-reading, quiet,
stick-in-the-mud who *was* my father, my *real* father.

He told me he truly believed that he had been at least
indirectly responsible for Admiral Dewey's great victory in
Manila Bay. "Now I'd been thinkin' about Manila Bay for
some time," Uncle Mike said. "And I knew in my bones that
Manila would fall like a rotten apple if only somebody in the
navy had a bit o' brains." He spat; I listened with fast-beating
heart. "Now all this happened, Gasoon, kind o' accidental-
like. Would ye keep it to yourself if I tell ye?"*

"Cross my heart!"

"Well, now, as I said, I'd been giving Manila a lot o'
thought, and this day I was havin' a lemonade in a San Juan
bar—after we took the town, of course—and standin' at the
bar right along side o' me was a navy man. We got to gabbin'
and it was then I sort of gave him the idea. Jist run enough
ships and big guns into the Bay, I says to him, and do it
sudden-like, and thim Spaniards will turn tail and run, I says.
All it takes is a bit o' boldness and Manila is ours, I says."

* "Gasoon" is Gaelic for "young one" and is generally used as a term of
affection.

Uncle Mike seemed at that moment to get bigger and grander than ever. I was hanging on every word.

"And do ye know what I learned later?" Uncle Mike asked. I could only shake my head.

"Well," he went on, voice lowered, "I learned that navy man was on Dewey's staff, by God! And he must've told the admiral what I said, because bedamned if the admiral didn't steam right into the Bay a month later and take the whole shebang, jist like I predicted!"

Struck dumb by this incredible revelation and bubbling over with almost insupportable pride, I gave Uncle Mike the tribute of my awed silence. A freight train rattled past. We looked up to watch, twisting our necks a little since we walked parallel with a high railroad embankment on top of which the tracks were laid. The last wheel clicked away; I stopped at the open end of a culvert.

"Over yonder," I said casually, "is where our deadly enemies hang out at night." I pointed beyond the tracks toward a large field; the culvert acted as drainage duct for this field during the heavy rains. Uncle Mike followed my gesture, frowned, and awaited further details.

"The Potter Street Pugs," I explained.

"Be they the young rascals yer mother is always consignin' to Purgatory?"

"They're bigger'n us and more of 'em," I said defensively.

Uncle Mike scrambled up the embankment and together we gazed over toward the big field.

"They come here nights and build bonfires," I explained.

Uncle Mike pursed his lips. "Oh, do they now?"

He teetered on his toes, big hands clenched behind his back and noble head lowered thoughtfully. At that moment, except for his height—Uncle Mike was taller—he looked exactly like the picture of Napoleon in our school books. I sensed he was absorbed in tremendous mental calculations and so I remained quiet. Abruptly, he strode down the bank. I followed. Uncle Mike stooped and peered through the cement drainage culvert, about thirty feet long, which cut through the embankment into the large field on the far side. He climbed back on the tracks again and stood there with his arms outstretched, turning slowly, somewhat like a weather vane. I felt a thrill of expectation. The arms dropped. Without a word Uncle Mike scrambled down the bank again—and again, I followed. I was winded. He jabbed a thick thumb toward the culvert.

"Can ye crawl in there, Gasoon?"

I crawled. There was plenty of room.

"Jist as I figured," Uncle Mike said solemnly. " 'Tis a perfect ambush!"

He explained the military strategy involved. Without doubt, he told me, the Pugs felt invulnerable, clustered around the big bonfire in the center of their field. *And*—he stressed this point—the moon rose over *there* (he gestured) in the east; ergo, the Pugs knew they could spot an impending onslaught, for the attackers would be silhouetted clearly by the moon as they came over the embankment.

"Now do ye follow me up to that step, Gasoon?"

I did. In fact, I was ahead of him.

"If we crawl through the culvert, they can't see us comin'!" I said with excitement. "And they'll be around the bonfire!"

"Right, me bucko! Right ye are!" He paused and closed one eye. "How many can ye muster?"

"My gang, that's five..." I counted. "Frank ain't old enough... and maybe five or six guys from around the neighborhood."

"Rally enough of yer force, hit 'em hard, then scatter!"

I was impressed at this brilliant piece of military planning and excited at the thought of giving the Pugs their deserved punishment. Uncle Mike had one final word of caution. "Ye won't, of course, mention a word of this to himself or yer mother?"

I crossed my heart and cast spit on the ground. He nodded, satisfied.

For a week I was busy with the gang in a council of war. Frank sat in on a couple of sessions but was given to understand that he would not be permitted to engage in our surprise attack. He screwed up his baby mouth, trying to look tough.

"I wanta go too."

"You ain't big enough," I told him flatly.

"Well, Davey ain't neither," Frank said.

Davey reared up and shouted, "I'm a year older! and I got two stitches!"

This was true. As ammunition-bearer, Davey had been conked only a few months ago, mostly because he couldn't take off fast enough, his blouse and pants legs being so weighted down with ammunition he was threatened with collapsed arches. Anyhow, by virtue of his stitches, Davey was a full-fledged member of the gang and since Frank couldn't answer Davey's indisputable claim that he had never been stitched, my brother shut up. He eventually lost interest in our meeting and wandered off, probably in search of something edible.

We gathered together another half-dozen kids, all victims at one time or another of the Pugs' depredations and more than willing to take part in the ambush. It was decided. We set the following Saturday night for the massacre.

Uncle Mike came down from Philadelphia that evening and took me out to the backyard. "How's the attack shapin' up, lad?" he whispered.

"Got ten men. We're ready to smash 'em." I never felt so important in my life.

"Now ye remember . . . attack whin the moon is jist comin'

up and crawl upon 'em without a sound! Thin, git to hell away from there fast!"

"Yes, sir," I said, "I'll remember."

Ten of us, loaded with stones, walked through the early dark. We approached the culvert cautiously. By prearrangement Davey was to enter first, signal us when he came to the other open end by hitting the side of the culvert with a stone. Hank, Nez, Moisha and I were to follow, in that order. If everything was okay, the other five were to bring up the rear.

Davey went in. It seemed to take him an awful long time to negotiate the culvert. The night was beautiful and calm, the sort of night that blended distant sounds with the soft whirr of crickets underfoot. I smelled hay in a cool wind, and the moon, a silver blur, hung over a chestnut tree. Finally I heard the signal. Hank went into the culvert, then Nez, then Moisha. My turn now. I crawled in. It was like entering, on hands and knees, a black tomb. Stars and crickets were blotted out. Moisha stalled and I bumped into his tennis shoes. The kid behind me muttered. I hissed and tried to push Moisha, who swore softly and inched forward again. Crouched low in the tunnel, I could feel concrete scrape my palm ... then suddenly the whole wriggling line stopped dead-still. There was an angry buzz of comment ahead ... and at the same time I was overwhelmed with an odor that hit like a hot blast. I gagged. I took a deep breath, held it, plunged ahead. In an instant I was wrist-deep and knee-deep in fresh horse manure. The stench was overpowering: rich, amniotic, gooey ... yards of it! My hands skidded, shot out, and I fell prone. Curses reverberated back and forth along the cement tunnel, and I found myself doing what those in the lead had done. I was up to my eyebrows in horse dung and, by gosh, behind me others were going to suffer the same fate! It was every man for himself, each stubbornly refusing to warn those to the rear. We were all in this, so that was that!

I tumbled out at last. For a few odorous moments all of us

huddled together, utterly defeated, thoroughly demoralized, and then the Pugs hit us in force. They emerged out of the dark, whooping, shouting, laughing like maniacs...we had walked right into their fiendish trap! One thought possessed us collectively as we clawed up the embankment, down the other side and raced home under a shower of stones. Unfortunately there was no way to avoid the main street of town, crowded at this time of night with Saturday shoppers and strollers. The breeze must have signalled our approach. Citizens smelled us from afar, sniffed suspiciously and stepped off the sidewalk to give us wide passage.

Several of the gang, principally Davey, kept up a continual fire of bitter comment as we trudged along, gripped in the double aura of disgrace and defeat. He stuck to my heels doggedly and expressed himself in no uncertain terms:

"Some uncle ya got, all right! Boy, what a general!"

"Shaddup!" Two women halted near a lamppost, wrinkled their noses and stepped off the curb as we passed.

Hank, too, became voluble. "Ya told us your Uncle Mike won the war, didn't you? Boy, was we dopey to listen!"

"Oh, shut *up!*"

Davey ran abreast of me and saluted with disdainful pomp. "Stragedy...yeah...yeah. Some stragedy...ambush 'em! Uncle Mike won the war! Boy, it's a good thing them Spaniards didn't have a mountain of horse apples..."

"I'll bust ya wide open...."

I told myself no one, not even my brilliant military strategist of an uncle, could have foreseen this terrible turn of events. Just the same, I experienced a skinking sensation... perhaps, only *perhaps*, Uncle Mike wasn't quite the military mind I had thought him to be...and I was grateful to Nez, who without taunting me merely growled occasionally and kept his head down. Moisha and the others seemed to be in a state of speechless shock.

It was Hank who eventually halted dead in his tracks and located the seat of treason. "Hey," he blurted, "didn't we have ten men?"

I wheeled around. I counted. There were only nine of us! A quick check revealed one kid missing. It was Chalky. We looked at each other while Moisha waved frantically, trying to find words. He knew something. We waited.

"His . . . his . . . h . . . hi . . ." Then in an angry rush he got it all out. "His folks moved t . . . t . . . today!"

So that was it! Chalky's parents had moved to another section of town . . . maybe, I thought, into the very neighborhood of the Potter Street Pugs. It was my first experience with a fifth columnist. It was unnerving. I was sure Chalky would go on in life to other resounding successes—he certainly knew how to look ahead.

Once in our own street we split and went our individual ways—Moisha wisely chose the cellar window to enter his house but Davey followed me right into my backyard, determined to hound me to the very door. Uncle Mike came forward in the dark, a hand outstretched.

"Did ye clobber 'em, Gasoon?"

I don't know what prompted me, but I stuck a sticky paw in his, and he took it. He jumped back as though stung. "The saints preserve us!"

Davey confronted Uncle Mike, his small form quivered with belligerency. "Ya . . . ya . . . general!"

Uncle Mike retreated a bit, produced a handkerchief and gingerly wiped his hands. "Seems like ye got out-maneuvered, eh?"

"*Manured!*" Davey yelled with disgust as he walked off.

Frank was at the kitchen table, chubby fists wrapped around a jelly sandwich. "Ya fall in sumpin'?" he asked brilliantly.

I chose to ignore him. Father was off somewhere and I

could hear Mother above us in her bedroom. I hurried up
to the bathroom, but I had hardly started to wash when she
appeared at the door. The odor stopped her cold.

"Glory be to God!" she gasped. "What now?"

"It was the Potter Streeters," I mumbled.

She sniffed and narrowed her eyes. "Now don't be telling
me they've taken to throwing *that stuff!*"

Lying on my bed and in the doghouse once again, a whole
summer later, I felt Uncle Mike had meant well ... how was
he to know that certain enemies don't fight fair, and how
could he foresee there would be treason within our ranks?
Yes, suppose some viper had tipped off the enemy at Manila
... would Admiral Dewey have been able to go through with
Uncle Mike's plan successfully? What would have happened
if—

"Come right down here, at once!" Mother's command
floated up the stairs.

What now, I thought? What new adult tortures?

Father's voice, louder that usual, took over as I came
downstairs through the living room into the kitchen. He and
Mother were in the midst of an argument, and I waited dutifully until they took notice of me.

"I'm perfectly capable of doing this myself, Sandy!"
Mother was insistent.

"Hush now, ye'll do no sich thing!" Father finally glanced
at me and went on. "Soon's I talk to the lad I'll go over myself."

"Oh, it's a stubborn lot men are, a stubborn lot," Mother
said.

Disregarding her tone, Father pointed his pipe at me. "Tell
me, lad, what might be the name of the leader of those
rascals yonder?"

"You mean the Potter Street Pugs, pop?"

"That I do."

"Well, it's a kid named Ashes . . ."

"Ashes be damned . . . I don't want nicknames! What's his surname?"

Mother intervened. "What's his last name?"

I took heart. They were talking to me as though I were actually a member of the family again. "Oh, they call him Ashes because his old man hauls ashes in that part of town."

"That's all you know . . . just that he's called Ashes?" Mother asked.

"Yes, ma'am." I edged toward a chair and sat down.

Suddenly Father became thoughtful. "B'jesus, wait a bit! I think I know who the lad's referrin' to! There's a rough-neck who belongs to th' Hibernians—name o' McGinty—hauls trash the other end o' town! His lad runs around with thim furriner Poles!"

Father was calm but his face had that expression it got when he was stubbornly determined about something and refused to budge. Mother made frustrated *tsk-tsk* noises.

"Now lad, I want to explain some facts o' life," Father said patiently. I sat up, alert. No question about it . . . events had taken a strange turn and I was out of the doghouse, my misdeeds apparently forgotten. "Ye'll learn," Father went on, crossing his legs, "that there's two ways mankind kin settle diffrinces of opinion . . ."

"Oh my!" Mother shook her head. "Will you listen to the man! It's over yonder in the Quaker pulpit they welcome such blarney . . ."

Father glanced at her. "Will ye let me talk?"

Mother merely repeated, "Oh my!"

"Ye'll learn, Gasoon . . ." Father cleared his throat ". . . that there's the way of violence—the ignorant fashion of doin' things—and the intelligent way."

"Hear the man!" Mother sat down and fanned furiously with her apron, but Father went right on.

"Yer Mother's gotten the foolish idea she kin go over to that neighborhood and berate some o' the mothers of those rascals—"

"Holy Mary, I've heard enough!" Angry now, she swooped Frank off the chair, half-dragged him off to bed.

Father waited until we were alone. "Women git pretty hotheaded whin their youngest is threatened," he said.

"That's right, pop."

"Oh, is it now?" He eyed me coldly.

"I was only agreeing, pop."

"Well now, suppose ye stop the blather and listen, eh?"

I decided to stop the blather.

"Now y' might as well git accustomed to the harsh facts o' life, lad." He paused and tried to get the pipe lit. "Ye've got to learn that *force* is *ignorance*."

He waited for that to sink in.

"Yes, pop."

"The world is changin', lad! The time is comin' whin there won't be all this violent way of life and men will see that it's a proposition of mind over matter, brains instead of bullets ... ye understand?"

I thought of Uncle Mike. Rather smugly, for it occurred to me that in my uncle's absence, Father had chosen me to test his theories. I sat up straight in the chair and tried to look intelligent.

"Yes," Father went on, "new ideas are takin' hold in the minds of men." He nodded with a satisfied air. "And I'll not be too proud to say it—one of the greatest of thim all is an Irishman and the intelligent people of the world are beginnin' to listen to his words."

"Saint Patrick, pop?"

"No. Paddy's long dead and the snakes with him. I'm referrin' to G. B. Shaw—socialist, philosopher and a great son o' the Sod." He sucked his pipe and blew out a wave of smoke. He frowned. Now he seemed dissatisfied. "Though why he's takin' to livin' in England, and him Dublin born, that I'll niver know...."

I wondered whether I could amplify my dinner with a second piece of pie and get away with it. Father was wrapped in his lofty thought. I reached out and captured a chunk.

"Yes," he went on sort of dreamily, "there's wisdom a'growin' and if ye strip the horny layers off the average man ye'll find a real peaceful soul beneath."

"Right, pop."

"Whin I took over the job bossin' that pack o' whiskey drinkin' moulders and coremakers, I tried first to drive them because they knew I could lick any man in the shop"—he caught himself—"that's if I wanted to, mind you lad, not that I actually wanted to...."

"Did'ja ever have to fight any of them, pop?"

He ignored the question. "I came to the conclusion the best way to handle men is the reasonable and intelligent way. Show a man you have respect for his intelligence and he'll work hard to prove he's worth your respect."

The pie slid down fast and I weighed my chances for another slab but decided no. A good thing, too, because Father came back to earth and stabbed the air with his pipe-end. "This gang o' hoodlums, now ... ye've got to keep clear o' them in the future."

"But, pop, they sneak around looking for us!"

"That's where this superior intelligence comes in!"

Nobody had ever accused me of that particular quality before; certainly Miss Pennypacker at school didn't hold any high opinion regarding my mental status. I was confused.

"Now, yer mother wants to go over and rant at the mothers o' those rapscallions...." Father paused to let me absorb the full significance of what he was about to say. "...But it's me who's goin' lad! I'll diminstrate how brains kin conquer brawn."

"You gonna wallop the Pugs?" I asked.

Father snorted and cast toward me a look of impatient scorn. "I'm beginnin' to think ye're as thick as yer Uncle Mike, bedamned if I don't! No, bejesus, I'm goin' to look up this Ashes' father and talk to him in an intelligent fashion. Once I explain to him what a danger to life and limb those little divils are, y'kin be sure there'll be an end to it!"

He shifted his glance to the dining room door, where Mother stood on the threshold, hands on her hips and wearing what Father often called the "O'Hara phizz," a way of looking sidewise-and-down-the-nose that denoted disdainful indignation.

"Rant indeed!" she said. "Don't think, Sandy Mullen, I'll soon forget these aspirations you've cast!"

Solemnly, slowly, Father rose and stood aside while Mother swept into the kitchen. Then he walked stiffly into the hallway to get his hat and coat. He knew better than to tangle with Mother when she was in a black mood. He'd often said, in lighter, more carefree moments around the house, that he could handle a hundred rugged locomotive builders with ease, but when Mother went on a rampage he always felt he must take to the hills.

"Intelligence...a man of peace, no less!" Mother's eyes flashed at me but her words were loud enough to carry out to Father in the hallway. "Sure, if certain parties within hearing distance think I don't know they *didn't* leave the old country in a leisurely fashion...but got out one jump ahead of the British..."

She walked to the door and made her voice even louder "...because a certain party within the sound of my voice was a Sinn Feiner and addicted to layin' in the dark of night with a shillelagh to vent his temper on stray Englishmen..."

The front door slammed. Mother sighed and told me it was bedtime.

It was still too early to sleep. I hung out the bedroom window and aimed my beanshooter at a flock of sparrows that swirled and chirped in the long summer dusk. Frank's face was buried in the pillows, and I was tempted to whang him on his fat rump with the beanshooter. I refrained, however. Mother, I knew, had ears on the back of her head.

The sparrows flew off, so I lay down and began to wonder if Father wasn't right after all. The Pugs were too numerous, too big, and far more battle-experienced than my gang. It started to make sense to me, the things Father had said, and I conjured up fanciful peace powwows with Ashes and his colleagues: *You guys stay out of our territory . . . we'll stay out of yours!* I envisioned myself striding dramatically into the midst of the Pugs grouped around their nightly bonfire near the railroad and overwhelming them with my superior intelligence—how they'd get red in the face with embarrassment and humiliation as I explained, in my lordly superior fashion, that gorillas and tigers are tough but really dumb . . . and after all, who wants to go through life being a dope?

About an hour later I was in profound conversation with that Great Son O' the Sod—that Irishman with the strange name, Jeeby Shaw. I, the World's Champion Peace Crusader . . . when the silence was suddenly exploded by loud laughter. It came from the kitchen and it was Mother's. Long, nonstop laughter that was too much for my curiosity. Barefoot, I crept down the stairs and peeked through the open kitchen doorway. Mother was seated on a chair, red-faced with laughter. Giggling and trying to speak which she couldn't on account of the laughing, she pointed at Father who was pawing around the open icebox.

"Now stop your silliness, woman . . . where the hell's that beefsteak?"

"Man of intelligence . . . brains over brawn . . ." She wiped her eyes with the edge of her apron. "I knew it! I felt it in my bones . . . oh, I knew I'd live to see this day!"

Father turned and I got a look: his nose was swollen and encrusted with gore; one eye was slowly turning all the colors of the spectrum. My father had been clobbered! Then I saw that the knuckles on both big hands were raw and I realized with a shiver of excitement that Father had also *done* some clobbering! He pulled a piece of steak from the icebox and slammed the catch. Still giggling, Mother helped him apply the red meat to his eye.

"Easy damnit . . . I'm that tender!"

Meat clamped to his face, Father was led to a chair, his head leaned back while Mother began to dab his nose with a wet rag. "B'jesus, I niver saw sich an ignorant man in me life!"

"Yes, Sandy," Mother said. The giggles were all gone but her eyes danced gaily. "And I'm sure he's worse off than you!"

"That he is, ye may be sure! It'll be some days before he can chew his grub."

"Yes dear. Now hold still."

"B'jesus, a man like that would try the patience of Job himself." He looked up at Mother with a supplication in his one good eye. "Now, ye know I'm not one to lose his temper easy, ain't that right?"

"Sure, Sandy—just hold still."

"I'm not a man to lie either, as ye know, but there's occasions and occasions, and whin I come home from the job tomorrow I'd like the Gasoon to believe . . ."

". . . that you got hit with a crane hook?" Mother giggled.

"Well, somethin, on that order."

I went to bed. Any story they might concoct, I already *knew.* What's more, I was beginning to respect my father.

CHAPTER VI

'Please Don't Take My Lovin' Man Away

If I miss the kiss
that brings me bliss,
Then I sigh . . .
Yes, I will sigh . . .
If I lose that hug
from my kissing bug
Then I will cry, cry
And maybe die . . .
I'm bound to go insane. . . .

Please don't take my lovin' man
away. . . . .

FATHER MADE ONE last desperate attempt to bring Uncle Mike to his senses. My uncle had come down from Philly and presented me with a baseball, bruised, discolored and a seam ripped.

"There I was, sittin' in the bleachers whin Ty Cobb of the Detroiters slammed this here ball right into me lap!"

My new-found respect for my father had by no means turned me into a cynic about my uncle.

I was overwhelmed with the present. Ty Cobb, no less!

Mostly because of his job, Uncle Mike got around considerably. He was proud of the fact that he was on fairly intimate terms with many of the great men in the world of sports; often he talked of what Bob Fitzsimmons said to him in the Diamond Bar, or what he heard Stanley Ketchell tell somebody else, and he'd say *if I took a drink every time a champean of th' ring or th' wrestlin' mat offered me one, sayin' Mike Boy-o have one on me, b'jesus, I'd never draw a sober breath!* And while he drank little besides his occasional bottle of ale, he affected the garb of the sporting man of the early 1900's: a deep curved derby; a hard, white celluloid collar topping a striped silk shirt; and from his gray vest there hung a heavy gold watch chain that seemed big enough to anchor a small sized vessel.

This particular Sunday Pretty Bess had arrived before him, which usually meant they had indulged in one of their spats. Uncle Mike had tried to kiss her when he came in, but he had to content himself with the offered smooth cheek.

My aunt daintily blew her nose, and I asked her if she had

a cold. Her eyes were teary as she swept me to her breast and hugged me. "Yes, it's a bit of a cold."

"It's this damp weather," Uncle Mike boomed. "It's bad for the weaker sex!"

"If it's weakness we'll be talking about," my aunt said stiffly, "it's no weakness of the mind like certain parties I could mention!"

"Now, Bess," Mother said, "it's the Sabbath."

Uncle Mike pulled open the bottom drawer of the dining room dresser and brought forth the ancient zither, a memento of my late grandfather, Old Dick O'Hara. He then went into the kitchen where he often played the instrument as exuberantly and casually as he did everything else. A moment or two later Father came in from a walk.

"Annie," he said, "there'll be a friend o' mine along for supper."

"And who might this friend be ... and why, pray, this sudden announcement ... not that I'm being nosey, mind you!"

"He's a draughtsman on the job, name of Corrigan."

"And that's all you have to say about the man ... while I have to entertain him on short notice?" She stood there, slim and beautiful in her long Sunday-best navy-blue skirt and her ruffled shirtwaist with the little etched gold watch pinned on her breast. From the kitchen came the inexpert plink of the tortured zither and Uncle Mike's rasping baritone.

> "Ohhh ... we'll stay no more
> on England's shore
> So let th' music play ... ay ... ay!

"God help us!" Father muttered. "Is there no peace?"

Pretty Bess placed napkins beside the dinner plates and stared at Father, a shy hopeful look in her eyes.

"Would this gentleman who's coming be having a thing or two to say about . . ." She hesitated.

Mother caught on, flushed and said with annoyance, "Yes, Sandy . . . would he be having anything to say about Alaska?"

"Well, now that th' subject's been mentioned," Father said casually, "that's jist why I invited him. I believe, matter of fact, that he spent three whole years in the Klondike."

Mr. Corrigan proved to be a rangy, red-faced man in his early thirties. Father introduced him all around. Pretty Bess sparkled. Mother was a bit offish, definitely suspicious, Uncle Mike abandoned his zither, came in and the big warm smile on his open features curled up and died when Father mentioned that Mr. Corrigan was somewhat of an expert on gold mining. Uncle Mike directed a searching glance at Father, who ignored it to pour drinks.

"Oh, he is . . . now is he?" Uncle Mike smiled again and slapped Mr. Corrigan on the back before that gentleman could utter a word. "Well, sir," Uncle Mike said loudly, "ye can help me no end and give me a few pointers. I'm off for the gold country meself soon!"

Father handed shot glasses to our guest and my uncle (nobody drank cocktails in those days, at least not in our house) and tried to edge the conversation in the desired direction. "Corrigan here"—he squinted an eye at Uncle Mike—"had himself the Devil's own time of it up there . . . ain't that right now, Mr. Corrigan?"

"Yes, indeed . . . you might say it was nip and tuck with the Grim Reaper himself. Why I remember the time—" Which was as far as Mr. Corrigan got.

"For th' life of me," Uncle Mike suddenly exploded, "I've been tryin' to figure who you remind me of, Mr. Corrigan!" He brought his big hands together with a whack. "Now, ye ain't by chance related to Bob himself, are ye man?"

Mr. Corrigan frowned. "Bob? I'm afraid I don't follow . . ."

"Why Bob Fitzsimmons, man! Quite a friend o' mine, Bob is!" He looked Mr. Corrigan over critically. "Have ye done any boxing, Mr. Corrigan?"

Our guest teetered on his toes. "No . . . that is, not professionally." He was pleased. "So I remind you somewhat of the great Bob Fitzsimmons, eh?"

"Ye do indeed!"

Mother chose that instant to call everyone to the table, and throughout the meal Mr. Corrigan hung on Uncle Mike's every word (tales real and imaginary) about famous prizefighters he knew, as well as jockeys and marathon runners, and at one point when Father tried to steer the conversation back to the Gold Rush of Ninety-eight and Mr. Corrigan's troubles and near disasters resulting therefrom, Uncle Mike countered quickly by throwing in a few weight lifters and famous ice skaters into the conversational arena. And as the big pork roast dwindled before the onslaught of seven hearty appetites, Father eventually became so annoyed that he began to strangle from, of all things, a mouthful of tea.

Mother pounded him on the back, a twinkle in her eye. "If you'd pay more attention to your food and less to Mike's sporting tales, you wouldn't be near choking."

"Or perhaps now"—Father coughed—"it's the Big Wind that did it to me!" He glared at Uncle Mike.

But Father never gave up easily. Right after the meal he took our guest and my uncle by the arms and steered them into the parlor "for our pipes and a nip or two."

The men were in there for about an hour. Finally Father exited by himself and walked stiffly into the kitchen, looking ready to burst. He poured himself a cup of coffee.

"I suppose," Mother said, "you had the Corrigan man in there put the fear of God into Mike, didn't you?" She shook her head sadly.

Father drank the coffee without a word. He walked to the

hall closet and put on his hat and coat. "I'll be taking a short walk," he announced.

"What's got into you, Sandy? We have a guest in the house!"

"Hah! It's Judas we have in our midst...not a guest!" Father left the house, slamming the door behind him.

Uncle Mike and Mr. Corrigan emerged a few moments later, my uncle's arm draped around Mr. Corrigan's bony shoulder.

"Well, girls," he beamed at Mother and Pretty Bess, "Mr. Corrigan bought himself fifty dollars worth o' stock in the Mullen Company. What d'ye think of that?"

My mother burst into laughter. Pretty Bess drew herself up once more, this time giving our guest her down-the-nose stare.

And that was the last and futile effort of Father to heave a wrench into the machinery of Uncle Mike's aborning venture. Resigned to the inevitable, Father and Mother decided to make a final gesture of family solidarity: a farewell party for Uncle Mike. As usual, for circumstances beyond my control, I was mis-blamed.

I moaned and threw my thin legs off the bed and sat up. My head lolled weakly on my stringy neck. Sheer hunger. *Agony*. I dropped to the floor with a thud, began to moan louder and louder until it became a sustained banshee wail. With great effort I managed to crawl across the room to the dresser and with more great effort, panting in gulps, I dragged myself up. I stared numbly at my image in the mirror and my head flopped sidewise, my strength gone. I was a prisoner. I was dying the most tragic death known to Mankind; a pitiful end to a blighted life brought about by starvation.

I heard Mother coming up the stairs and I dove back on

the bed with alacrity. She opened the door and stood there, hands on hips.

"What," she sighed, "are you up to *now?*"

"I'm hungry," I said.

She threw up her hands. "Now you had a breakfast big enough to choke a horse!"

I remained silent, I was in bad enough as it was.

"And if you think you can scheme your way out of this house today after all the devilment you got into..." She departed, muttering to herself.

Hearing the clamor of fire bells, I ran to the bedroom window, leaned out as far as I could without falling and caught sight of the Hanley Hose Company steamer tearing down our street, white-helmeted firemen hanging on grimly to the apparatus (which looked like a huge gleaming Thermos bottle standing upright) while two beautiful white horses galloped toward the blaze. Farther down the street I could hear the excited hoots of kids who, somehow, miraculously always managed to arrive at the scene on the heels of the fire horses. My gang would be there, minus a couple of that morning's casualties, while I had to remain a prisoner in my room...just because the Katz goats did a nutty thing and didn't know how to behave like a team of Huskies. And, I thought grimly, I was the fall guy, as usual. I came away from the window and glanced at myself in the dresser mirror. I was bored stiff. The image looking back at me wasn't pretty by any stretch of the imagination: a scrawny red-headed boy of nine whose two front teeth were overlarge and whose face was covered with freckles the size of a dime. All this was topped off by a thatch of hair that seemed to be made up exclusively of cowlicks. I whipped out an imaginary Colt .45 and shot him dead in the mirror. Then I flopped back on the bed. I got blamed for *everything*.

I swore to myself that I would leave home that very night

after everybody was asleep and I would make my way up to Alaska and never come back again. I'd get two six-shooters and scare all the baddies out of the goldfields so that Uncle Mike could get his gold mine working, and then we would bring the gold back together and when Mother got down on her knees and begged me to forgive her, I'd say, "Why did you treat me so cruelly and make me leave home and get behind in my school lessons?" I conjured up a mental picture of how Mother would react when she found I had left home. She would stand there, the tears running down her face, and she would finger the little gold watch she wore pinned to her shirtwaist and she would sob. "Why was I so mean to my dear little boy? I'll never see him again!" And my father would put his arms around her and say, "Now, now, Lady, he's a good boy and he'll come back to us."

Eventually I got tired of that and began to read the pile of old funny papers on my bed. I went through about three months of "Little Nemo" for the umpteenth time—that wonderful little fairylike character was my favorite—and then I perused a batch of "The Katzenjammer Kids."

There was an increasing rattle and bang and hurried footsteps downstairs and I knew it was Mother getting the house ready for Uncle Mike's farewell party . . . the party I simply could not miss.

Father wasn't expected home from the Baldwin works for at least another four hours and sometimes when he arrived he wasn't in the best of humor. I wondered how he would react when Mother told him of the day's events and my part therein. If he were feeling pretty good and not too tired, he would listen to Mother respectfully until she finished and perhaps he would say, as he often did, "Well, does the lad have all his arms and legs, Annie?"

"Of course he has! Now don't make light of me, Sandy!"

"And I take it, then, he's still alive?"

"Sometimes I wonder how he manages to stay alive! You treat that boy too gently, Sandy. Now you have a talk with him, the scamp!"

There was a racket on the stairs and I recognized sounds only Frank could make. There was a clatter and a thump where he missed a step and fell back down. He resumed. Clump. Clump. Stomp. Silence. The door opened cautiously and I glared as he came in. Frank, still cursed with a Buster Brown haircut that Pretty Bess had wished on him, was chewing a big gob of black asphalt tar. His pudgy knees were a network of raw red scratches.

"What do *you* want?" I demanded. If it hadn't been for Frank and that nutty Moisha, I wouldn't have been incarcerated this important day.

"Pretty Bess is here," Frank said, looking at the floor.

"I know, nutty, I know!"

He wanted to talk, to get back in my good graces. "Pretty Bess is crying. Pop says Uncle Mike makes her cry."

"Pop's just a stick-in-the-mud," I said, a fickle admirer. "Uncle Mike is going to bring me back a gold mine."

Bess came in, red-eyed, and kissed us both; her pompadour was smooth and her dress pretty but her mouth was sad and I felt awful—just awful. Everyone was either about to be jailed, or crying or—I looked at Frank—hanging around where he wasn't wanted.

Hours passed, very slowly. This time I recognized the feet on the stairs at the first step. Heavy, aggressive, strong. The door swung open. "Hello, me buckos!" Uncle Mike shouted. "What kind of devilment have ye been up to—getting the police after that poor furriner next door?"

I experienced a sinking feeling. "I was mis-blamed," I said. "Will they arrest me too, Uncle Mike?"

Frank wiped his nose on his sleeve. "It's all my fault," he said.

Uncle Mike poked him with a thick finger. "Ah, now, ye're good lads, both of ye . . . if the police come, I'll tear them limb from limb."

"How did you know about it?" I asked.

"Oh, I have a way with your mother," he laughed. "She gave me a quick account of your latest doin's and I must say, lad, this one's for the books. Where did you get the idea that harnassing goats to a galvanized washtub could turn them into huskies?"

A thought struck me. "Can I go to Alaska with you, Uncle Mike?"

He seemed to consider it seriously, but he shook his head. "Well, maybe after I get the mine workin'. But right now I want to see himself when he comes home from work. After all, I can't have a real bang-up farewell unless you're there, can I now?"

He went back downstairs to wait for Father. I felt much better.

Frank was deep in thought, one cheek misshapen from the gob of tar. He looked at me sorrowfully. "He tried to kiss her but she wouldn't let him."

"Who?"

"Uncle Mike. Aunt Bess," Frank said. "She's real mad at Mike."

"You shut up about Uncle Mike."

"Mom made apple 'n' cherry pies," he said. "I'm going next door to tell Mr. Katz it's all my fault."

"You stay away from the Katzes." I pulled my knees up under my chin and brooded.

Uncle Mike was right on the job when Father came home. I could hear them downstairs and amid the rumble of deep voices, I heard my father shout, "He *what?*"

I couldn't hear Uncle Mike's reply, although by that time I was hanging over the banister to catch the drift of things. I could tell Uncle Mike was really pouring it on in my defense, though. A moment later, back in my room, I heard Father ascend the stairs and I breathed a sigh of relief. If he had been thoroughly angry he would have run up, two steps at a time.

When Father flung open the door, Uncle Mike was behind him. He winked at me. I waited. Father was brief.

"Do ye want to end on the gallows?" he asked without preliminaries.

He had been shaving; now he frowned and slung the towel over his shoulder. As I've said, Father never really walloped me—the worst I ever got was a careful boot in the backside when he wore his carpet slippers—for he was a powerful man. Standing there with his shirt off, his arm muscles were huge and his chest and back were massive knots of sinews.

"I've got a mind to make ye sell newspapers and shine shoes to pay for wrecking that washtub!"

Even though I was the victim of an atrocious injustice I agreed this was what I should do.

"I'll start working Monday, pop! Gee, I'm sorry about Mr. Katz—"

"So ye will, eh?" Father cut me off. Then he did the thing that always puzzled me in those days—he got angry all over again about something that was not really connected with the basic problem at hand. He turned to Uncle Mike. "D'ye hear th' lad?" he shouted. "Threatenin' to go out and shine shoes!" Now his voice was loud enough to be heard downstairs. "Ye'd think he didn't have a father who can clothe and feed him!" He shook a finger at me. "Now, enough of that kind o' gab! D'ye hear?"

"Yes sir," I said meekly.

Uncle Mike leaned on the dresser, twiddled his fingers. "Louder, Sandy! She'll think you're assassinatin' the boy."

"And I'm beginnin' to believe," Father said, "th' child's as scatterbrained as ye are!" He stalked out. Uncle Mike winked at me and followed Father.

I had been reprieved.

I descended from my doghouse, my tread quiet, my expression angelic. Mother chose to ignore my existence. I spoke to her several times, attempted to act offhand, but she didn't answer me. Aunt Bess, aproned and rosy, was mixing enough doughnut batter to feed a regiment. For the party, my mother had a twenty-pound ham, clove-dotted, sputtering in the stove; occasionally she opened the oven door and basted it in its own golden juices. Pans of fresh-made bread sat on the back of the stove covered with white towels.

We ate supper in the kitchen and when we were finished a wagon drew up from the Vogel's Bottling Works. Uncle Mike helped carry in three cases of ale he had ordered, the driver dropped off a fifty-pound cake of ice, and my father contributed six quarts of Irish whiskey. He drank very little ordinarily, but Mother admonished him not to get what she called a "skin-full" at the party.

When the dishes were put away Father looked around and asked, "And where's the addlepated Croesus, may I ask? Him with the gold inlays in the brain?"

"Hush now," Mother said, "they might hear you." She gestured toward the parlor where Uncle Mike and Pretty Bess were talking behind closed doors. "You may as well take it with good grace, Sandy. This is Mike's last night with us for a long time."

"It could well be the last," Father said. "The toes of dead men are sticking out of the ground all over Alaska."

The moment arrived that Frank and I had eagerly awaited. Father lugged the ice cream freezer up from the cellar, where it reposed under canvas. I was given the task of turning the crank ... after Mother poured in the country cream, the fresh pineapple, the sugar. All this done without once speaking to me. Frank hovered around, eager for his turn, and we churned away. Intermittently we peeped into the slowly congealing ice cream and, when no one was looking, we tested it with our fingers.

When we finished with the cream Mother deigned to speak to me for the first time that evening. "Air the room," she said, looking at me as though I were some foreign insect.

The phrase "air the room" had special significance in our household. What it entailed was preparing the front room of the house, the parlor, for a special occasion. The parlor was always kept closed, the windows down and the furniture covered, except for parties, funerals (we had buried grandfather Dick O'Hara from the front room several years before) and momentous family conferences. Otherwise the folding doors barred the parlor from humanity for weeks on end and all objects in the room were kept carefully polished, dusted, scrubbed or covered. I had never seen anything in the room so much as an inch away from its accustomed niche or position.

In this room, under lock and key, Father's many books were stacked in a large oak chest. A bell jar covered a cluster of wax roses that stood between the two windows facing the street. These windows were kept shuttered except for said special occasions. On the yellowed marble mantelpiece stood an ormolu clock, which always reminded me of a toy house, all black and brass with marble columns. The big sofa was hard, and if you leaned an elbow on the arm rest the protruding horsehairs jabbed you. Three petit-point footstools, featuring lancing knights on stately horses, sat in front of three ponderous easy chairs, which were anything but easy to sit in. There was a large gilt-framed print of Christ over the mantelpiece and directly across the room, over the Lester piano, hung a plaster crucifix, also gilded. There was an immense curved glass-front bookcase containing volumes of Marie Corelli; *A Romance of Two Worlds, Sorrows of Satan, Barnabas,* the *Complete Works of Mark Twain* (these Father bought for Frank and me) and a beat-up assortment of Guy de Maupassant. There was also a stereopticon with lots of slides. Among my favorites were pictures of the Chicago World's Fair, the "Scenic Beauty of Lush Hawaii," and a set of our naval fleet. The two lower shelves were used to display tiny porcelain knickknacks Mother had collected. The bookcase was always locked.

A three-foot bronze statuette of the Winged Mercury stood in another corner. It irked me that Mercury seemed to be going somewhere like a bat out of hell, but every time I saw him he was still in the same position.

With Frank as my assistant, I yanked the slipcovers from the chairs and sofa, folded them neatly and put them under the sofa. Then we unhooked the inner shutters and threw the windows wide open. The air was sultry. We pushed the folding doors back, hooked them to the walls, and I turned on the three wall gas jets and lit them, making sure the delicate mantles were not broken. That was part of my responsibility. I also had to wind the ormolu and set it with the dining room clock. After ten minutes, we closed the windows: the parlor was ready for guests.

The first to come was Uncle Aloysius, who gave me a pat on the head and asked me how I was getting along in school. Mary, his brown-haired wife, had baked a big chocolate cake for the party, and as I helped her lift it out of the box I managed to knock a hunk of the thick chocolate off the side. Frank popped it into his mouth before I could gracefully reach for it, and after making due apologies for my clumsiness I glared at Frank and muttered a warning. He swallowed and cast his eyes down.

Uncle Aloysius lost no time in heading for the dining room, where Father and Uncle Mike had opened a bottle. A severely dressed and sad-appearing distant cousin of my mother's, Miss Kate, from Philadelphia, was the next arrival and then several women friends of Mother's. The women all congregated in the parlor, the men in the dining room.

The smell of fresh-baked ham drew me to the kitchen, where Pretty Bess, her slim form wrapped in a flowered apron, cautioned me against any piratic thoughts I might have. "You'll get plenty to eat when it's ready!"

She weakened, smiled conspiratorially and gave me a slice of the ham just as Mother appeared in the doorway. "Bess O'Hara . . . you've puttered out here long enough. Come into the parlor."

My aunt shook her head. "I'm all right here, sis. *Somebody* has to keep an eye on things."

Mother heaved a great sigh, and I wondered what was wrong. Women were such strange creatures. "Bess, do cheer up a bit! A body'd think this was a wake, not a party."

Pretty Bess wiped her hands on the apron, compressed her lips. "I'll have you know I've already had a sufficiency of sorrowful advice from a couple of our guests . . . I want no more!" Her skin seemed to darken in anger.

"Who now?"

"That Kate Murphy for one . . ." Pretty Bess mimicked the seldom seen third cousin from Philadelphia. "To be sure, she made a point of telling me I am 'still young and have the best of yer life ahead!' " She uttered the last words in a cloying sweet falsetto. "You'd think I was burying Mike instead of bidding him a temporary farewell!"

"Ah now, you are too sensitive. I'm sure Kate and the others meant well," Mother said.

"Meant well indeed! They merely meant to tell me I've been . . ." she swallowed and the word came with difficulty " . . . *jilted!*"

"Bess O'Hara, I'll listen to no such talk!" She sounded angry. "We've been over this time and time again! Mike is doing what he thinks best . . . Mike is doing this for *you*, girl!" Then she impetuously put her arms around my young aunt. "Mike loves you, Bess."

"He certainly has a peculiar way of showing it!"

"Come to the parlor. The neighbors are beginning to arrive."

"I'll be in later," Pretty Bess said. Then, mostly to herself, "When the acid has finished dripping from their tongues!"

She would not come to the parlor and Mother knew it. She bit her lip and went back to the women.

Bess suddenly realized I was near the stove. "You scamp! Someday I'll pull those big ears—" I fled into the dining room.

Here the table had been widened to its maximum by the insertion of table leaves; it was gigantic and on it sat a veritable feast: sliced turkey, chicken, pork, a dozen small cut glass bowls of pickles, jellies, olives; fresh-baked layer cakes and pies ... all this waiting the addition of the big ham Pretty Bess was at the moment slicing in the kitchen. Uncle Mike, Aloysius and Father sat at one end of the table surrounded by trays of glasses, large and small, around which—like doomed soldiers ready to die—stood an array of bottles— whiskey for the men, wine for the ladies. There was enough to drink ... hard liquor, claret, and out in the shed bottles of dark ale that floated among chunks of ice in a galvanized washtub. About thirty people were expected that night— mostly neighbors, with a sprinkling of kinfolk. Father and my uncles were uncomfortable in their celluloid collars, and occasionally one or the other would grimace and run a finger between the rim and the neck. They were drinking Irish whiskey, and a strained conversation was under way when I arrived.

"Aye, and I wish ye were comin' with me, Al," Uncle Mike said.

Father studied him over the rim of his drink.

"Two years back I would have, Michael bucko." Uncle

Aloysius laughed. "But I'm a married man now. Hitched."

"Roped," Uncle Mike said softly.

"How's that again, Michael?" Uncle Aloysius blinked.

"Now don't be misunderstandin' me"—Uncle Mike reached over and prodded him in the ribs—"yer Mary's a fine woman . . . there's naught finer around . . . she's a comely lass and it's a lucky man ye are, Al . . . but . . ."

"But what, man?" Uncle Aloysius' tone was edgy. Father placed his glass on the table and folded his arms. He said nothing. Uncle Mike had that casual air I admired in him—a Man of the World.

"Now I'm not holdin' with thim radical friends o' your'n," Uncle Mike continued, "I'm a God fearin' man meself. . . ."

"Git to the *pint* and stop shilly-shalling," Uncle Aloysius snapped.

"Well," Uncle Mike drawled, "irregardless of what I think about yer friends' ideas of lockin' horns with the British Crown . . ." he paused and quickly crossed himself ". . . and His Holiness, I'm thinkin' ye should've took a crack at it . . . if only fer the good o' yer conscience!"

Uncle Aloysius was slow to anger, but this was too much. "Jist what'n hell are you insinuatin', man? And what was that wise observation about me bein' roped?"

"Ye were hornswoggled into the bonds o' holy matrimony" —Uncle Mike glanced at Father—"at th' instigation of himself here!"

Uncle Aloysius banged his whiskey glass on the table.

"I'll have ye know nobody hornswoggled me . . . and I resent the implications of yer remarks!"

Father spoke up. "It's yer own brother you're defamin' and I'll thank ye now fer an apology!"

Uncle Aloysius nodded violently at Father's intervention and with deliberate movements began to take off his coat.

"And if he don't apologize, I'll be put to th' unwillin' task o' beatin' th' b'jesus out o' him!"

Father got to his feet. Uncle Mike remained seated. He flicked ashes from his black cheroot.

"All I'm alludin' to," he said, "is what ye know to be God's own truth, Al."

At this point Uncle Aloysius began to roll up his sleeves with meticulous movements. Father placed himself in a strategic position, glanced from one to the other and awaited developments.

"Keep right on with yer insults," Uncle Aloysius said hoarsely, "because in one minute I'm goin' to do violence to yer person!"

Uncle Mike poured himself a drink. Nobody paid any attention to me as I watched all this open-mouthed.

"Ye're me own flesh and blood, Al." Uncle Mike sipped his drink. "And all I'm tryin' to convey to yer thick skull is this . . . I feel sorry fer ye! To me dyin' day I'll believe ye were outwitted, b'jesus! Jist as himself here tried to outwit me and keep me from goin' up north!"

Uncle Mike spit on his palms and performed a little dance. Father grabbed him. "Easy man! Easy!"

"Let me poke the ugly phiz o' him!"

"Now there will be no brute force permitted in this household," Father said firmly. Uncle Mike looked at me and winked. Father pushed Uncle Aloysius into a chair, and it seemed to me he was awfully easily persuaded. Then my father muttered something about Cain and Abel and poured drinks all around. Uncle Aloysius brooded over his, and Uncle Mike drew hard on his cheroot and made a perfect smoke ring for my benefit.

Pretty Bess, appearing with a platter of ham, took the situation in at a glance. "I heard a ruckus in here! If certain parties would act as though they had manners . . . hard put though they may be . . . I'd like to say there's an old lady just come in the back way and I can't get her to go into the parlor."

"Would she b'chance be placin' herself near the tub o' ale?" Father inquired.

"She did, indeed," Pretty Bess said.

"That'd be Miss Louella, th' sewin' woman," Father said. He turned to me. "Lad, go bring your mother." He turned to the others and finished his drink. "Lady has a good heart for them that's afflicted with weaknesses o' the flesh."

Mother retrieved Miss Louella from a too-close proximity to the ale tub and brought her into the parlor. The house was beginning to fill up with guests when Mrs. Katz came in from next door. I tried to avoid her eyes, but she wagged her head sadly at me and smiled. She had brought a large covered pot of triangular meat-and-cheese-filled kreplas and Mother thanked her and asked where her husband was. In her halting English, Mrs. Katz explained that he had a very bad headache and had sent his apologies. Mother withered me with a look and took Mrs. Katz into the parlor to join the other women.

The menfolk centered in the kitchen and the dining room, where there was the Irish whiskey and the bottles of ale. In the parlor the women, dressed in fluffy shirtwaists and their hair in pompadours, were hard put to maintain ladylike airs as the evening wore on, trying to make polite conversation and at the same time to keep an ear cocked toward the rear where my father, my uncles and menfolk from the neighborhood who had been invited were getting noisier by the minute. Frank was shooed off to bed at nine and at ten Mother began to move in my direction with the same purpose in mind when there was a sudden, unexpected hush in the men's department. Mother and Pretty Bess looked at each other, then —at once—hurried in that direction.

Uncle Mike had his chair tilted against the wall and his shiny brogans were propped on the table; in his hand was a half tumbler of whiskey. Uncle Aloysius smoked a long-stemmed clay pipe and gazed dreamily at my father. Mr.

Knowles and Mr. Webster, parents of my friends Nez and Hank, likewise stared at Father who stood in the middle of the floor, a sheet of notepaper in his hand. Mother and Aunt Bess halted in the doorway and waited. Father weaved ever so slightly, then regained his balance.

"I'm addressin' this poem"—he squinted at the paper—"to a certain party present at this memorable occasion." He listed a bit and looked pointedly at Uncle Mike. "This's from the pen of a great poet—one Thomas Hood, b'name."

"Hear, hear!" Uncle Mike said, a bit thickly.

The other men nodded politely and tried to appear sober. Father held the paper close to the gaslight on the wall and began to recite, his voice heavy with emotion:

> "Gold, gold, gold, gold.
> Bright and yellow, hard and cold.
> Molten, graven, hammered, rolled
> Heavy to get and light to hold,
> Stolen, borrowed, squandered, doled."

Father carefully folded the paper, prepared to launch into a profound lecture on lack of stability and its dire consequences —for Uncle Mike's benefit—when Mr. Knowles interrupted the proceedings. Father coughed politely and gave way. He was host, after all. Mr. Knowles rose to his feet a bit unsteadily and took off on a loud rendition of "Dangerous Dan McGrew." He drew a round of applause when he finished. He bowed and collapsed in his chair. Father cleared his throat and prepared to pick up where Thomas Hood left off. But again he was thwarted, for Mr. Webster, perhaps inspired by Mr. Knowles, rose and quavered a pet rendition of his own: "The Face on the Barroom Floor." By the time he finished— this also accompanied by loud applause—Father snorted and gave up. He poured himself a stiff drink of Irish.

Bedtime finally came and Uncle Mike went up to my room

with me. There was a hard lump in my throat, and now that the time of parting had come I realized I loved him deeply, maybe even more than I loved my mother and father, if that was possible. Uncle Mike did a rare thing that night. He kissed me. We sat on the edge of the bed and he kept his deep voice low so that he wouldn't waken Frank.

"Ye believe in me, don't ye laddie?" he whispered.

I nodded and was afraid to speak, afraid I might start to bawl.

"That's good," he said, sitting there in the moonlight that shone through the window. "Whin ye grow up, I want ye to have a college education. And I don't want you or Sandy or yer mother or Pretty Bess ever to want for a thing!"

He was silent for a while. Frank snored gently. "I want the whole damn family to have silks and satins and pockets bulgin' with money." He stood up. "Now keep yer nose clean while I'm gone, lad!"

I crawled under the covers and after he left I cried—I couldn't help it. Eventually I went to sleep. Sometime during the night, the sound of sobs wakened me. Father, for once, hadn't been able to navigate the stairs, so Uncle Mike had bedded him down in the parlor—and I knew Pretty Bess and Mother were in the next room. I heard my mother trying to soothe her and I again wondered at the strangeness of women. Why couldn't Bess realize that Uncle Mike was doing this for everybody? Why shouldn't she want the sables and the Pierce Arrow he would buy her when he came back, laden with gold. Some party!

I turned over and fell asleep again.

CHAPTER VII

Shenandoah

O Shenandoah, I long to hear you . . .
Away you rolling river. . . .
O Shenandoah, I long to hear you. . . .
Away, I'm bound away . . .
Cross the wide Missouri.

O Shenandoah, I love your daughter. . . .
Away you rolling river. . . .
For her I've crossed the rolling water . . .
Away, I'm bound away . . .
Cross the wide Missouri . . .

Up toward the end of our street was an old house, flanked on one side by a large plot of lawn on which there was an ancient peach tree. The area between a broad stone walk and the house was a mass of perennials. Miss Pierce, spinster, occupied the house. The neighborhood saw little of her except on summer nights when she sat in a rocker at the window.

Every year we observed the budding peaches with intent longing. And not a summer went by without our gang raiding the tree under cover of a soft, warm night; chunks of sawed-off broomsticks, hurled into the branches, were sufficient to bring down the booty. Although Miss Pierce was hard of hearing, some intuition would invariably warn her of our wraithlike presence and she would lean out the window and berate us.

One very warm June, Miss Pierce was taken sick and an old man came to our neighborhood carrying a big cloth suitcase. I heard Mother tell Father at supper that the newcomer was the older brother of Miss Pierce and had come from upstate to be with her during her illness. He was a tall, bony man with a stern blue eye and a black patch over the other. His tanned face was rimmed with a close-cropped white beard and a mustache. The patch was kept in place by a silken string that looped slantwise around the back of his white head. That patch intrigued us. I recall how we stood near the iron fence outside the Pierce house and talked it over. My friend Nez Knowles said: "He's one of them pirates."

"Hah! He's ... he's ..." Moisha began, but we ignored him, knowing it would take forever for him to untangle his words.

Hank Webster said: "Aw, he probably got his eye knocked out by a Indian war club!"

That sounded as ridiculous to me as the pirate theory, but I felt obliged, too, to endow the mysterious old fellow with some equally colorful halo, so I compromised. "He ran out of bullets and was wrestlin' with a wild buffalo ..." I volunteered, but my friends hooted derisively before I could finish. By mutual, unspoken agreement, we dropped the subject and went off to set traps for muskrats down near the river. A few days later we observed from a distance that the peaches were nearly ripe and we decided to stage a raid that night. The one-eyed stranger, we figured, wouldn't know about our annual looting, consequently we were a bit careless when we climbed over the iron fence and heaved our shortened broomsticks into the branches. Without warning, the old man materialized right in our midst, swept a whistling circle with a rattan cane and gave me a sharp wallop across the bottom. Moisha got it, too. Yelping with anguish we flew over the iron fence and ran up the alley behind our row of houses; Moisha whimpered a stuttering lament, both of us rubbed our stinging wounds. Hank and Nez, who had escaped the cane, hooted their delight. We held council. The peaches were more desirable than ever, and I remember as we discussed the problem how my mouth watered at the thought of them. Now it had become a worthwhile *project*. Our task was clear; we simply had to devise ways and means to outwit the old man.

The next night we changed tactics and climbed over the wooden fence in the rear of the Pierce house. The old man, we calculated, would watch from the window and expect us to come over the fence in front again. Our plan was brilliantly conceived. We would approach the booty circuitously and heave our clubs into the branches from behind the shelter of a weather-beaten tool shed in the yard, situated obliquely out of sight of anyone at the window.

The plan worked beautifully in its initial stages. We threw the clubs up into the tree, the noise muted by a soft wind that rustled the thick-leafed branches. When we had downed enough fruit, Hank crept forward on his belly. In the dim moonlight we could just about discern his shadowy form in the high grass. Then all hell broke loose. A clatter of numerous bells shattered the quiet night. I almost jumped out of my skin. Hank rose out of the grass like a skinny phoenix outlined by the silver fire of the moonlight, yelling with fright. We got away from there fast, and as I went over the fence I saw the old man, lantern held aloft in one hand and cane in the other, walk down the yard. When we gathered together in the alley a few moments later, the sharp clang of bells still echoed painfully in our ears.

Hank's teeth chattered. "I was creepin' along just fine," he said breathlessly, "and then I ran into this kinda wire . . . and when I tried to pull it aside, all them bells started to ring like tarnation!"

The old man had strung a wire barrier around our peach tree. Hidden by the tall grass, the wire was attached with an assortment of clapper bells. Twice now, he had outsmarted us. We began to view him with downright awe—and enmity. To be whipped by Our Deadly Enemies, the Potter Street Pugs, was one thing; to be outwitted twice in a row by a mere old man was preposterous. Now we *had* to make a successful raid on the peach tree. Our honor was at stake.

Two days before the eagerly awaited Fourth of July we tried again. This time we put all our intellectual efforts into the task. It *had* to be foolproof. That day I went up on the roof of the last house on our row and peeped down into the Pierce yard. The wire and bells were still in place. I could see

the four short sticks (which the old devil had taken the pains
to paint green!) supporting the wire and bells, the whole contraption hidden by the high grass. I made a mental diagram
of the trap.

That night we again entered the Pierce yard from the
rear. We had rehearsed every phase of the raid. I crept first,
bellywise, and the other three slithered along right behind
me. The night was on our side; there was no moon. The
Pierce house was black and silent. Ever so carefully, I crept
forward like a cautious ant, probing gently with my hands
as antennae until I felt the wire. I whispered to Hank, next
behind me, and he felt the wire. All four of us now located
it and got over without jiggling a bell. We were elated.

Then we proceeded with Phase Two of our strategy. We
didn't dare heave the sticks up into the branches lest they fall
and hit the bells. I stood upright, put my arms around the
tree and Moisha climbed on my shoulders and swung himself
up into the tree. Nez went up next. Everything was going
according to schedule, but we really hadn't estimated the
Machiavellian potential of our enemy. Without warning we
were collectively hit by a deluge, a gigantic swirling cloud-
burst. Moisha and Nez tumbled down, spluttering. Hank
whooped and fled and I followed him in a dive over the fence.
Once more, we found ourselves in shameful retreat, this time
to the accompanying jibes of the old man who had hidden
himself in the tool shed all the while. We had arrayed ourselves like four clay pigeons, and the old man had quickly
opened a valve on the lawn sprinkler he had hooked up in
the branches of the tree. A miniature Niagara had hit us.

Back in our alley, gasping and shamed, we were a bedraggled foursome, indeed. I was a marked man, for this latest
foolproof plan was of my devising. Nez took off his soaked
pants, wrung them out furiously and departed with his usual,
"T'hell, with it, men!" Hank threw me a murderous look and

he, too, left the scene. Moisha sat collapsed against the high alley fence and swore volubly in Yiddish, either at me or the old pirate . . . or both. I decided to go into the house and try to forget the whole affair.

The Fourth of July came in with a roar. In those days there were no restrictions on the sale of fireworks and the whole population celebrated with voluminous, earsplitting bangs. As with most kids, our gang had saved, snitched, worked for and connived pennies and nickles weeks in advance for the purchase of fireworks—red and white torpedoes which, when thrown violently on the sidewalk behind an unsuspecting victim, exploded with the impact of a .45 caliber bullet; red jumbo firecrackers that you set off inside a big washtub or an oil drum; Roman candles that swooped skyward in arced beauty and split the heavens with a thunderous crack. Every kid arose at the first glimmer of dawn on those long ago July Fourths, and when we finally staggered off to bed at nightfall we resembled pale, begrimed infantrymen of modern wars who have gone through major engagements. Our mothers had to shout to make themselves heard, for we were ear-numb and battle-fatigued.

But this particular July Fourth was of special importance. There was to be a military ceremony at a cemetery on the outskirts of town, where the dead of the Civil War and '98 were buried. So our gang went over to the Town Square early and watched the uniformed veterans arrive from all over the county.

The center of the Square was jammed with the men of two wars. The veterans of '98, booted and wearing colored neckerchiefs and broad tan hats, mingled with scores of much older men who wore forage caps or wide-brimmed, dark blue officers' hats trimmed with gold and silver insignia—Civil War soldiers who had fought at Chickamauga, Gettysburg or The Wilderness. All around us was the blaze of silken regimental banners, tall tobacco-chewing men greeted each other loudly—and amid all this, our eyes were held by the glitter of officers' polished swords. I even coaxed a Civil War cavalryman to let me hold his saber. He unhooked it, wide belt, scabbard and all, and handed it to me with a smile. "Think you could swing that there weapon, sonny?"

It was amazingly heavy. I said, in all seriousness, "Gee, mister, only a giant could swing it!"

And when he buckled it around his waist he smiled and said, "I hope you never have to, I sure do!"

Somewhere a bugle blared, its golden tones clear and decisive. The ranks began to form. Then, away up ahead, there came the deep roll of drums and the veterans of two wars began to march to the cemetery. The air was clear and warm and the bright sunlight awakened the faded colors of the blue uniforms and the soiled, torn banners, and glinted on the iron-blue rifle barrels and the long, thin, fluted bayonets. We fell in behind the last line, keeping step to the staccato, clipped rhythm of the drums up ahead.

Eventually we arrived at the burial grounds. Hundreds of townfolk were already there, many of them descendants of those who rested under the rows of small stone markers, each topped with a small new flag. Soon speeches were being made by men attired in civilian clothes, but our gang paid them no attention; our eyes were transfixed by the sight of the soldiers who stood in solid ranks in rigid attention, rifles at their sides while the flags fluttered lazily in the gentle summer breeze. There was a strong, heady odor of roses that lay like a blanket of peace over emerald grass and the white stones of the cemetery. Roses were everywhere, and wild ones bloomed in riot on the low stone wall in the background. The graves of the war dead were banked high with fresh-cut gardenias and roses donated by the townfolk.

Our attention was centered on the ranks of troops when

we saw our Old Nemesis. He came toward us in a long-legged, booted stride, passing down the front ranks of the Civil War veterans, one hand clutched on the hilt of his cavalry saber, the other gauntleted and swinging. Gold-braided epaulets shone from his broad, bony shoulders. He wheeled, stepped back, facing the ranked troops and barked a command in a hoarse voice. The soldiers snapped into action. As old Pierce shouted commands, the rifles rose up into firing position and the quiet summer air was shattered by a salute to the dead. We stared at old Pierce, tongue-tied with surprise. There came more sharp commands and the soldiers wheeled and marched off. Nez grabbed my arm and pointed. The old man had walked over to one of the graves, his brimmed blue officer's hat in one hand, and he stood there for a moment, tall, immobile, his head slightly bowed. He stooped and picked up a stray rose and put it back on the grave. Two younger soldiers wearing the jacketless Spanish American War garb walked up behind us. They were talk-ing. "Yep, that's Pierce! Pennsylvania Bucktails! That's him for sure!" It was apparent from the tone of respect that our Old Nemesis was somebody special. "The only Yankee that Stuart's Raiders was afraid to tangle with! And he sure as hell cut the Rebs to pieces at Shenandoah!" Then another said, "Ain't many of them kind left," and they walked away.

Old Pierce put on his hat and strode off. I caught a glimpse of his features. He looked sad, not at all menacing. Later, when we caught up with the soldiers now headed back to the Town Square to disband, we felt much better, for our recent defeats by old Pierce now took on an immeasurably greater meaning: a Civil War *colonel*, the man whom the fabulous Jeb Stuart feared, had taken the trouble to engage *us* in a battle of wits. For the next few days we said little about the colonel and we kept away from the Pierce yard, for there was no question now of another raid.

About a week later, we sauntered past the yard and cast a

yearning glance at the tree, now heavy with luscious peaches. It was night. Someone called from the shadows of the yard. We stopped, hesitant. Colonel Pierce emerged from the shadows and came to the gate. He seemed tremendous as he stood there in the bright moonlight. But he was grinning.

"You fellers give up kind o' quick, don't you?" he said. There was a portentous silence. Hank spoke up.

"Yes, sir. We know when we're licked."

Colonel Pierce banged the gate with his cane, punctuating his laughter.

It was Moisha who acted. He stepped forward, faced the old warrior and drew his thin body erect. He saluted. The colonel's bearded face went solemn; he hung his cane on the fence and returned the salute. The rest of us, experiencing the strange dignity of the moment, found ourselves joining in the salutation.

"At ease, men!" Colonel Pierce said. Our hands went down.

We turned, as one, and walked off into the moonlight. From the darkness, as we strode away, came a low rumble of laughter. I turned and saw the colonel's straight old form fade as he walked back to the house. We felt good now. Hostilities were over. We might have been defeated, but we had been treated honorably as worthy opponents.

CHAPTER VIII

Home Sweet Home

*Mid pleasures and palaces though
         we may roam
Be it ever so humble
            there's no place like home....
A charm from the skies
            seems to hallow us there....
Which seek thru the world
            is not met with elsewhere.*

It was early afternoon. The sidewalks were fiendishly hot to bare feet, so we decided to go swimming.

We sauntered down to the river. To our chagrin we discovered that our usual spot on the riverbank had been expropriated by our deadly enemies, the Potter Street Pugs. About a dozen of them disported in the water, having left a guard to watch over their discarded clothing. Anyone who swam and was foolish enough to leave his raiment unprotected would inevitably find the raiment dunked and tied into a Gordian knot.

We stood off a safe distance, and perhaps because it was hot and they were disinclined to think, my colleagues looked to me for instructions. I spoke with terse authority. "We're outnumbered men. Let's go up the river aways."

Hank, my old partner-in-crime, surveyed me with disgust. "Ahh, I ain't afraid of them if you ain't!"

Davey and Frank stood by loyally, waiting for someone to issue a battle cry. Moisha clenched his thin fists and stuck out his lower lip, indicating *he* was ready to tangle with the Pugs, if no one else was.

"It's hot," I said.

"Yeah." Nez merely shrugged confirmation. "T'hell with it, men!"

Abandoned by Nez, the rest of the gang acted like foot soldiers in battle who suddenly realize their heavy artillery is no longer available. I, meanwhile, chose to ignore Hank's innuendo, which clearly implied I had developed a yellow streak. Nez and I started off in search of a suitable swimming spot. The others grumbled and followed. About a mile upstream we found a good place; our flank was protected by a swamp of cattails and reeds, and the tough-bladed grass along the river bank was as green and sweet as the water itself. We wouldn't need a guard in that isolated spot. We disrobed —a simple matter indeed, for all we wore in hot weather were a pair of short pants. Summer days were spent bare-chested and barefooted, the exception being Moisha, whose mother made him wear an oversized pair of tennis shoes because, in addition to his difficulty in enunciating, he was also extremely nearsighted and might walk on glass or nails without shoes. (He was instinctively farsighted, though, and could see the truant officer six blocks away.) So, unencumbered by underwear, socks and such nonsense, we simply slipped out of our pants and dove into the water. An hour or so later Moisha, who was trying to perfect his Australian crawl, spluttered and shouted, "Hey ... loo ... loo ... looka ... "

I looked toward the shore. A big hawk had swooped down on our clothes. From long experience we knew that hawks were mean-tempered and larcenous; for the sheer hell of it, they would swoop down on a paper kite and rip it apart or, if you took a puppy to the river, you really had to watch the hawks, for they were known to fly off with a small helpless dog. This one, however, had spiraled down on our heap of pants. Before any of us could swim to shore and heave a rock, the bird was aloft, and we knew that one pair of pants was rapidly disappearing toward the blue horizon. As one, we reached the bank and went to investigate. Somebody was pants-less. We were a good three miles from home. A quick inventory revealed that Frank was the victim. As we stood in a dripping naked circle over the heap of remaining pants, I'm sure we presented the sort of picture that would have evoked ecstatic meter from a Whitman or a Housman: bare bodies glistening under the bright afternoon sun, muscles sleek and resilient, hair water-soaked and shiny, clinging to skulls in shades of red, blond and black.

Actually our unpoetic expressions of opinion at that moment would have been more suitable for review by the juvenile probationary authorities.

We had a problem. Obviously Frank could not walk home three miles on a sunny afternoon naked as the day he was born. I looked at my brother. He stared back with absolute trust. As the oldest, I had better come up with the solution. I fought back a feeling of frustration and turned to Hank. He screwed up his freckled face. Nothing. Next, I pinned Moisha with a questioning look. He shrugged. Nez, from his expression, was ready to dispatch the entire situation to hell. I ignored Davey deliberately because I knew he would merely suggest that Frank saunter home in the raw. Hank was the fastest man in the gang. I studied him and he knew what was on my mind.

"Aw, it's still daylight!"

"How'm I gonna get back for supper?" Frank demanded.

"Get to the first backyard you can find," I instructed Hank.

"I told you, it's still daylight," Hank argued.

"Grab anything," I ordered. "A sheet ... a towel ..."

Reluctant and surly, he took off. It was an hour before he returned, so red-faced from exertion we didn't even *ask* if he had been chased ... it was the foregone conclusion. His booty was a suit of man-sized BVD's. Not good, but better than nothing. We concentrated on the back-flap first. Moisha found a rusty nail and we pinned the flap. Then we put the underwear on Frank, which hung fulsomely in all directions and reached down to his ankles. Thus garbed, he would attract as much attention as he would strolling around stark naked.

I had an idea. In summer the high school track team often

ran through the streets of the town. However the trackmen had numbers on their backs. Another problem! Then Nez produced a kitchen match, made a small fire of driftwood and with a piece of charcoal drew a large "$12\frac{1}{2}$" on the back of the BVD's. I rolled up the droopy legs. Moisha's oversize tennis shoes had to do as track sneakers. Frank put them on, took two steps forward and fell flat on his face. It took some time before I taught him to run properly by lifting each knee high, in a sort of trotting-horse fashion. This, I hoped, would keep him upright and prevent the BVD legs from dropping down to his ankles. Finally he got the point. We put on our pants and started toward civilization, occasionally calling a halt to roll up the lower portions of Frank's underwear. When we reached the outskirts of town, I instructed my brother: "Don't stop to answer any dopey questions . . . and don't stop until we're home. Head for the alley."

Off he went in the lead. We loped along about a half block behind. Now and then, as we approached the more thickly populated areas, people would turn and stare, but Frank puffed valiantly ahead, heedless of the curious. We had to cut across the main street to get to our neighborhood. The gang trotted behind Frank as he approached the busy thoroughfare. He held to the center of the street and wagon drivers slowed to watch him pass. He was halfway across the main street when disaster struck. I saw him swerve, falter and come to a dead halt. An ice wagon veered to avoid hitting him. I skidded to a barefoot stop and so did the gang as the full portent of the calamity struck us all.

My mother, shopping bag in hand, stood rigid as she watched her rotund offspring standing in the middle of the main street of town, one BVD pant leg dropped to his ankle. The other rolled up on a fat leg. With unerring mother-instinct she swept a frigid look in my direction. I made a frantic effort to dive behind a vegetable bin outside a store. It was too late. She saw me. Passersby halted, startled at the sight of a plump redheaded, strangely garbed child with a Buster Brown haircut who had brought traffic to a halt. I saw Frank cast his eyes down and then glance covertly at Mother. In his six-year-old innocence he must have decided that Mother was horrified, not at him riveted in the center of the thoroughfare, but at the ungainly raiment he wore. Whatever passed through his mind in those tense, hectic seconds I'll never know, except that he *did* decide to make amends to my mother by clumsily unbuttoning the front of his BVD's and, before Mother's agonized shriek could stop him, letting them drop in a heap at his feet ... then he stepped right out of them. Mother flew into action. Horses reared as she rushed toward Frank. A sizable crowd watched the rescue and the comments were mixed: They ranged from uncontrolled laughter to the prim disapproval of several women who let it be known—in loud tones—what they thought of *some people and their children.*

I observed it all with fast pulse and parched throat. Moisha chose that moment to stutter a meaningless wail and sat down on the sidewalk beside me with a hard thump. Then his pinched face held a puzzled smile and he fainted. I ignored him. I wished I could pass out myself. Life, I knew, would be unbearable from here on in, if not longer ... and, as always in a crisis, the rest of the gang—Hank, Nez, Davey—had disappeared, swallowed up in the crowd.

Mother snatched up the oversized BVD's and dragged Frank along by one ear, trying futilely to drape his plump form with the flapping underwear. I closed my eyes and refused to watch. It was hot on the sidewalk, and as I knelt beside a vegetable bin I suddenly had visions of vast expanses of Arctic snow ... and a red-and-white-striped North Pole ... and I yearned to be far away with my Uncle Mike —away from it all—the laughter, my mother's anger, the heat.

I hung around the streets ... mothers called to their kids,

the streetlamps came on, and still I didn't want to go home. I had often enough graced the interior of the doghouse but invariably I slipped out within a comparatively short time. This occasion, however, was in a class all by itself. I knew Mother. While her understanding of my countless misdemeanors might seem limitless, and it was true she was fiercely proud of her family and defended us and even boasted a bit now and then of *her* sons, *her* husband . . . the sight of *her* beloved Frank standing bare-bottomed naked in the center of the town's main street, in view of several not-too-kindly disposed women friends . . . well, this surely was beyond the pale. The very least I could expect would be not a few days, but several weeks of dire penalties. These would surely include, I knew, a cessation of the weekly movies (no Pearl White serial at the Nickelodeon); absolutely not a crumb of her wonderful chocolate cake; chores to do all day, every day (wash and dry the dishes, clean shoes, take a bath *every* night, run errands . . . on and on). All this to the audible accompaniment of my friends outside, as free as young eagles.

It was after nine o'clock when I rounded the corner of our street and slunk toward the front of the house. As I expected, Mother was seated on the front stoop, fanning herself. The night was really quite cool. She sat upright and rigid. Stealthily, I detoured and flew down the back alley; with utmost caution I pulled open the back door, and there sat Father. For a moment I thought I had been outflanked. I waited. He smoked his pipe and watched me.

"Kinda late, eh?"

"Yeah, I guess it is."

"You didn't eat? You've not been cadging food from the neighbors now?"

"No, pop."

"Hmm. Seen yer mother?"

"I saw her, but she didn't see me," I mumbled.

His sharp blue eyes held me transfixed. "Women'll suffer anything but public embarrassment. You ought to remember that."

"I'll try, pop."

"Ye sure did it up brown this time, lad!" He rose and listened intently in the direction of the front of the house. Without question Father had assumed one of his neutral positions for this dreadful affair. He seemed downright worried. I remained dutifully rooted to the spot as he tiptoed toward the big stove. He reached in and brought out a pie pan with two immense fish sandwiches, then he handed them to me and admonished, "Now git this grub down and don't git crumbs on the bed!"

I wasn't hungry. But he seemed to expect me to do or say something—I didn't know what, and anyway my throat was closed up tight, so I took the food and scurried upstairs.

Frank was in bed and fast asleep. I shoved him over, a little contemptuously—even if he was only six years old he ought to have more sense than to choose the center of town in broad daylight to pose naked! I remembered Mother's face and swallowed hard. Mother even opposed the usual practice of the kids swimming naked in the Delaware. She had stern notions about modesty, and although I knew she was aware that we often *did* swim in the raw, I knew also that she chose to ignore this, realizing perhaps that she couldn't patrol the river daily during the entire summer. Father was noncommittal on the subject.

Frank rolled over and muttered something about forty-eleven apple pies. How simple everything was for a six-year-old! I personally felt I had fallen into a deep, deep black pit. Life was horrible, I decided. Plain awful. The stair treads creaked and I shoved the fish sandwiches under the pillow ... then the door opened a little and I could see my mother's outlines against the hall light. Ordinarily she would come in and kiss Frank and she would rumple my hair to say good-

night. I waited. She stood without moving, face implacable
and stern. I coughed. The glance she directed at me convinced me that I was no child of hers at all, just some kind
of biological accident she refused to acknowledge. The door
closed and she was gone.

No food, no punishment, no goodnight. I had reached a
terrible milestone in my young life, a crossroad that demanded drastic decision on my part. I wouldn't stay another
minute in this house! I had to leave home. At once I went to
the dresser and found the compass I had traded Hank for
a hefty wedge of cold potato cake, filched several weeks ago
from Mother's pantry. It was a white celluloid affair with an
uncertain pointer, but I would need it to make my way away
from home and out into the wilderness, eventually to meet
up with Uncle Mike. Moving quietly because of Frank, I
unscrewed the brass knob of a bedpost and drew up the
Bull Durham tobacco bag in which reposed my hidden treasure: thirty-one cents in dimes and pennies, the change
mostly contributed by Aunt Bess. I took a pillowcase from
the bottom dresser drawer, quickly loaded it with my extra
pair of shoes, some underwear, stockings, and a pair of corduroy britches. On top of everything I placed the two big
sandwiches. I located my jackknife with its one broken blade
and I was ready.

Father was still at the kitchen table reading. He glanced at
me and put aside his book. The kitchen was hazy and the
oil lamp on the table fluttered, but I knew that neither rain
nor blizzards nor wolves nor drowsiness could interfere with
what I had to do.

"What in the name of sanity are ye up to now?" Father
asked in a whisper.

"I'm leaving, pop." I also kept my voice low.

He crossed a knee, leaned back and sighed. "Oh, so ye
are, eh?"

I nodded.

"Well, lad, if it's not askin' too much ... man to man like ... jist where are ye headin' fer?"

"North, I guess. Maybe Alaska."

He frowned and sighed, no doubt once again cursing his brother Mike for not only his own foolhardy adventure but now for putting outrageous notions in a young innocent's head as well. "And do ye be knowin' how far that is?"

"Yes sir. It's up at the North Pole."

He nodded and pursed his lips. We still talked in whispers. I reached into my britches and showed him the compass. I felt a bit sorry for Father just then because I realized he never traveled and probably didn't know how to use a compass.

He examined it thoughtfully, handed it back. "Well," he said, "I suppose there comes a time in every man's life whin he must leave his bed and hearth."

"Yes sir," I said.

Father rose, walked to the back door and looked out into the starry summer night. He spoke with his back to me. "Ye won't be sayin' farewell to Mother?"

"No sir. I don't think so. She's kinda mad."

"That she is, to be sure." He sighed, opened the door and shook my hand, solemnly and gravely. "Well, lad, the best of luck!"

I walked down the alley with my belongings and I wanted to bawl. Everybody made everything difficult. I felt so miserable I even forgave Frank his nutty striptease ... poor Frank ... poor Pop ... my throat tightened as I realized that I might never again see my family ... and behind me I heard the Katz goats bleat. Then I visualized how shattered Mother would be when a Northwest Mountie rode all the way from the North Pole with the terrible tidings that my frozen body had been found, clasping my jackknife, surrounded by dozens of wolves I had killed before I succumbed to the fierce blizzard that eventually snuffed out my pathetic and tragic young life, and I felt better.

It was late and the streets were almost deserted. I passed Mr. Knowles swaying down the sidewalk, humming "Rock of Ages" in an off key, and a little farther down I thought I spied Miss Louella West. Most of the houses were already dark and the streetlamps seemed uncertain. I checked my compass and assured myself that north lay where it should. Our town was small and made a semicircle on the Delaware, the flat side along the river, the curve touching farms and open fields. I knew that a half-hour walk would bring me to the outskirts, so I plodded onward, shaking my head once in a while to clear away the drowsiness.

The sidewalks ended and there were no more backyards. The night seemed blacker than any night I'd ever seen, and the air—soft and warm—was filled with muted cricket song and at times with hollow noises that had an ominous ring. I stopped again and consulted the compass. Assured, I went on. Then the moon ducked behind a cloud and I could feel my heart pound behind my ribs. Nothing but black... a tremendous wolf bayed mournfully, dismally... I shivered, my knees trembling until I finally identified the sound as that of a dog in a nearby farmyard. At home, Frank would be dreaming of food... Father bent over his everlasting book... and Mother, maybe she was making lemonade? I was thirsty. The dirt road curved to the left and everything seemed alive —shadows moved, the trees hissed, the grass in the fields wiggled—and I almost walked into a gigantic grizzly bear that loomed a few feet ahead. I dropped the pillowcase and gasped, my legs refusing to obey a command to flee toward home.

Suddenly the skies lit up in a wave of heat lightning and I saw it was no grizzly... only a huge lilac bush. I staggered over and sat down. After all, I thought, I hadn't eaten my supper so it was reasonable that I should stay and eat one of Father's sandwiches. I took it out of the pillowcase and began to munch. Down the road was a blob moving closer, closer

... this time it was a gorilla—broad, powerful and ominous. I peered into the dark, my mouth full of fried fish and bread. It had disappeared! Shaken, I crawled into the bush and forced my way into the mass of thick roots, dragging my belongings with me. The food stuck, I could hardly swallow. I had to outwit the gorilla. I knew something about them. Once Father had taken me to the Philadelphia Museum and I had never forgotten the horrible black-bellied gorilla that stood in stuffed, snarling menace before visitors who stared, shivered and moved away. Gorillas, I knew, inhabited countries with trees, and that's where I was now—trees all around —and such monsters that could tear a man limb from limb. I had to hide and wait. I pulled the stuffed pillowcase into position and made it as compact and comfortable as possible. It might be a long time—I wasn't too sure of the nocturnal habits of jungle animals. I laid the compass on the ground beside me, I could feel my eyes get heavier and heavier....

The sun lit my bedroom with dancing shafts of gold. I lay, uncomprehending, my mind fuzzy with a dream where I had been picked up by a gorilla and carried, helpless and dazed, in its powerful arms. I could feel its warmth ... smell a strange tobacco odor on the night air.

Home!

I sat upright in bed with fright and relief. I was home! Had I dreamed it all? No, I knew I had run away. I had talked to Father.... He was funny, I decided, and even if he was a bit of a stick-in-the-mud, even if he had almost talked Uncle Mike out of going to the Klondike and coming back with a barrel of gold, even if he wasn't brave and adventurous like my Uncle Mike and read books when he didn't have to ... he was a swell guy, my father.

The day before's events crowded into my confusion. Frank naked. Sneaking home. Packing the pillowcase. All of it. Beside me Frank snored gently and over the soft rumble I heard the doorknob turn as Mother came in. She was smiling, a little thoughtfully to be sure, certainly not her usual open smile . . . but she *was* smiling.

"Up now, the both of you. Time for breakfast!"

Frank leaped from the covers, fresh and rosy-cheeked. "What we got, mom?"

"Pancakes this morning. So hurry now." She picked up my dirty sock, shook her head, and went out.

I was flabbergasted. She had smiled! We were having pancakes and it was only Saturday. We never had pancakes on weekdays. Frank made for the bathroom where he would, I knew, perform his split-second turn-on-and-off of the water tap and lightning swipe at his face with the towel, all in a matter of less than thirty seconds before sliding into his clothes and all but tumble downstairs to get to the table. I rose and dressed in dreamy leisure, making everything last as long as I could. At the breakfast table, when I reached for a pancake and forgot to use my fork, Mother whacked me sharply. And she even spoke directly to me. "Will you ever learn manners?"

The situation was normal again.

CHAPTER IX

I'm the Lonesomest
Girl in Town

I'm the lonesomest gal in town,
Everybody has thrown me down. . . .
I ain't got no angel child to call me dear . . .
Got no honey man for me to cuddle near. . . .
Yes, I'm the lonesomest gal
In this here town,

PRETTY BESS CONTINUED her regular weekly visits. Mother was content, Father took a new book out of the chest in the parlor, and there came a Sunday when, had I not been so inexperienced with the wiles of young womanhood, I might have tumbled to the fact that Pretty Bess had not abandoned her schemes; she had merely cleverly switched tactics. She paid particular attention to me on this occasion and about an hour after she arrived, I caught her discreet whisper: "Go up to your room. I have a surprise."

Mystery! I loved it. A little later, alone in the bedroom, my aunt materialized with the surprise. A box of decalcomanias, absolutely taboo as far as Mother was concerned. Strictly forbidden! I was enthralled. Spread on the bed there were over a hundred of them: raffishly colored little papers that you licked, pasted on an arm or chest and then pulled loose, leaving on the flesh a gorgeous picture precisely like a tattoo . . . there were heads of Buffalo Bill, Abraham Lincoln, Sitting Bull, George Washington, in addition to gold-and-blue emblems of our army and navy plus large curlicued initials and whatnot.

"Gee, they're great," I said, "but what about Mom?"

She smiled conspiratorially. "Put them on outside the house but wash them off at night before she sees them."

That seemed a terrible waste, but I saw the logic of it.

"And, if she catches you," she cautioned, "don't say I gave them to you! Agreed?"

I nodded, examining each of the stickers carefully while I pondered which one I would try first. Bess smiled, tweaked my ear affectionately and waited until I had gathered them into a neat pile.

"Can you keep a secret?" she asked. "Please now, it's got to be a *real* secret, Gasoon. Your mother or father must *not* know."

"I hope to cross my heart and spit!" I swore.

"All right then! Here's what I want you to do . . ." She opened her purse and extracted a dollar bill. "Take this. Without letting your mother know, go to the Five and Dime and buy all the noisemakers you can." She hesitated, then took out two additional dollar bills and handed these to me also. "Next Saturday afternoon round up all the kids you can and go to the afternoon show at the Nickelodeon . . ."

My head whirled. Kazoos, racket makers, horns . . . then take my gang and any other kids I could round up . . . and that wouldn't be hard! I must have looked blank because Pretty Bess went on to explain in a whisper that she had finally entered the elimination singing contest to be held at the Orpheum Theatre in Philadelphia the last week in August. The winner of our local contest would receive five dollars. The final victor would win *two hundred more.*

"The one who gets the loudest applause wins," Pretty Bess said pointedly. "And remember, I don't want you to breathe a word of this to your parents, understand?" Bess went to the door. "Not . . . a . . . word!"

I realized, of course, that Frank would have to be excluded from this deal, mostly because he was too young to appreciate secrecy. Nez, Hank, Moisha, even cynical little Davey could be trusted, however; and in addition there were any number of highly experienced noise experts among my school chums who would willingly—nay, frantically—join me on Saturday.

The week dragged by and it seemed that Saturday would never come. Still, Friday rolled around at last . . . the day before the big event. And then the Big Day of the contest arrived. The mothers in the neighborhood must have felt that Saturday morning that every boy had suddenly been stricken normal—well, perhaps not exactly normal, for they knew their offspring were on the verge of illness if they miraculously ceased to climb, wrestle, and produce noises like a mass dogfight beside a roaring fast-freight. Grimly, I went about the performance of every task assigned to me by Mother: I washed the parlor windows, tidied my room till it resembled the meticulous interior of a monk's cell; I went to the grocery store for the week's supplies and didn't dawdle for an instant, returning with the exact change of a five-dollar bill. I swept up the litter in our tiny backyard and, glancing at the kitchen clock to find there was still plenty of time before the Nickelodeon opened, I nobly gathered my shoes together and polished them to an intense glitter. This last act caused my mother to stop her chores, sit down with a thump and consider me with baffled wonder. I maintained a dedicated air, spit on a shoe and whammed it energetically with the brush. Mother rose and stared at me incomprehensibly, then went about the task of rounding up Frank for his Saturday bath.

I had given Hank, Nez and Moisha the responsibility of gathering a claque; I had two dollars for admission (a nickel each) and we were to muster up to forty strong, armed with the various mechanisms of noise that we could clip at the last minute in the Five and Dime.

At one-thirty I disappeared from the house while Mother still tried to scrub Frank down to his natural hide, and I was not the least surprised to find my gang—plus fifteen kids from our immediate vicinity—all on the alert for the Money Man. We had expropriated five twirling ratchets and five shriek-producing tin horns for a dollar, distributed them (they were promptly tucked under our shirts) and then trooped into the theatre.

The first portion of the show was confined to the usual run of amateur performers; they merely competed for the regular

Saturday matinee prize of five dollars. Amateur shows in those days drew spectators not much different from the Roman mobs who hoped for, and got, blood. It took supreme courage for an aspiring trouper to get up on one of those stages. They *had* to be good or else in the midst of a rendition—be it a tap dance, an acrobatic feat, a comedy act, a song or an eager harmonica arpeggio—they might be knocked flat by a swooshing sandbag that swung pendulum-fashion across the boards from a rope or they were in danger of getting "The Hook," a long, insidious pole with a beribboned hook on its end that stole out of the wings toward the victim —slowly, slowly—and snatched him or her off the stage with embarrassing dispatch. Such ungainly disposals were based entirely upon audience reaction. Once the chant began... *the hook ... the hook ... the HOOK!* it was all over.

After a half dozen such casualties the manager appeared on the stage, held up his hands and brought the audience down to a relatively sated purr. He announced that the next four attractions, while amateurs, were to be treated with dignity because this was the much-talked-about contest whose winner would wind up on the Philadelphia Orpheum stage in competition for the grand prize. "*So please,*" he urged, "*your kind attention, ladies and gentlemen!*" I fingered my horn and wondered where among the four Aunt Bess was scheduled. The first contestant was a perspiring young man who twice started off in one key while the small piano player chose another. The audience maintained a deadly quiet. The young man, apparently under normal circumstances a deep bass, was trying to sing "On the Road to Mandalay," but when he eventually started *on* key, and abruptly once again departed from key just as dawn was coming up like thunder, the audience could not contain itself and thundered him right off the stage.

He was followed by a pert young lady who simulated the chewing of gum and was dressed in a slinky split skirt and an enormous wide-brimmed hat. She twirled a red parasol. *She* was cool despite the swelter of heat within the theatre and the piano player, at her confident nod, began "Frankie and Johnny." The girl could sing, there was no doubt about it. She fluttered her mascaraed eyes and all the while walked in short little swaggers back and forth, showing her front and posterior profiles to great advantage. When she finished, the crowd broke into a roar of approval. I felt a hollow in the pit of my stomach.

Next was my Aunt Bess. At first I didn't recognize her. She was heavily rouged and lipsticked (rarely had I ever seen her with even face powder) and her long dress of white fluffy lace was set off by a white hat with ostrich plumes. The hat! (I was to learn later that Uncle Mike had been inveighed into springing for it as a peace offering before he'd gone off to seek his fortune—much to mother's exasperation. I liked to think, privately, that my desperate effort to get the precious hat for her had somehow inspired Uncle Mike, though I'd never actually told him about what fine motive lay behind our disastrous assault on the pickle vat earlier.) Aunt Bess was a lovely picture, so much so that I got up and glared angrily at some fresh guys who shouted, "Oh, you kid!"

Bess was also, even I sensed, nervous, and I almost curled up and died in my seat. I perspired, felt my throat go dry and wanted suddenly to be away from there. If anything happened to my young aunt...if the crowd hooted...I'd catch the next freight train and never come back.

Now Pretty Bess took a deep breath and smiled. I felt better. Then she held her hands out toward the audience, began to measure off a beat, and the piano commenced. Her voice was rich and tantalizing as she sang a new Irving Berlin number, "When I Lost You."

When she'd ended her song, all of the claque let loose simultaneously. It was earsplitting. Even so, we hardly needed it. The crowd almost tore the roof off and Aunt Bess had to do an encore, even though the manager rushed on the stage and tried to head it off, shouting, "This is not fair, ladies and gentlemen ... there's another contestant ..." The audience clapped and stomped and demanded Bess until, reluctantly, the manager nodded. Bess leaned over the footlights and spoke to the piano player. Then she sang one of her favorite songs, "I'm the Lonesomest Gal in Town."

The final contestant didn't have a chance. It was another young man, and though he tried halfheartedly I'm sure he realized the prize was in the bag. Which it was. With much ado, the manager appeared again, lined up the four singers for applause and Pretty Bess won hands down. With a flourish, the manager counted off the five dollars, in new dollar bills, just about what Pretty Bess could earn in a week singing at the Five and Dime.

I tried to catch my aunt's attention but she seemed so excited I gave up. As we filed out and went back to our neighborhood I briefed my gang once more on the absolute necessity of secrecy. I was satisfied. I was sure she was, and I felt even closer to her as a result of the happy results of our conspiracy.

Now Father was an honorable man, but like certain gentlemen of the more distant past—Brutus and Cassius to name two—who tempered their honor with chicanery, he was not above resorting to low-handed tactics if he believed these actions were for the good of everyone concerned.

It was a night just a few weeks after the contest, and I had just sneaked in the front door when I was arrested by voices in the dining room. Mother and Father sat at the table and from their tone I gathered something unusual was afoot. They whispered, then they argued, then they went back to whispers again. Curiosity overcame caution, and I stood in

the dark hall and listened. It had to do, I discovered, with
Pretty Bess and Uncle Mike. Anything that concerned Uncle
Mike especially interested me, so naturally I eavesdropped.

"Now I know what I'm doin', lady! I've studied the matter
and I'm usin' what Shaw calls a *psychology* ... and fer your
information, it's a new way to bait a hook so will ye be quiet
fer a moment?"

I peeked around the archway and saw Father lay down a
pen, push aside some stationery and hold up an envelope.
"I'll take the trouble to explain once again," he said. "I enclose
this stamped, self-addressed envelope in this letter I'm sendin'
to th' Fairbanks police. I'll ask the police up there if they
know the whereabouts of Mike. Now de ye git that straight?"

"You needn't be so testy, Sandy!"

"Well, all right now! Thin the police up in that forsaken
country sends me a reply ... in *this* envelope ... the one I
stamped and self-addressed." He beamed with satisfaction.
"If I say so myself, it's ingenious!"

"I don't know, Sandy," Mother said, "I don't like it. It's
dishonest ... why, it's forgery!"

"Look ye, woman! Whin I give the returned envelope
postmarked 'Fairbanks, Alaska' to Bess ... and she reads a
letter and *thinks* Mike wrote to us ... it'll git her over the
foolish notion of goin' up there to find him." He glowered
at Mother. "And fer that I'm called a dishonest man!"

"I hope it works." She rose and kissed Father on his head.
"If Mike would only come back ..."

"Aye, it's a long time," Father agreed.

"Send it then," Mother said abruptly. "I suppose you're
right. We have to do something ... anything ... yes, send it!"

All this, I must confess, puzzled me. I went upstairs,
washed, and crawled in beside Frank, who rolled over and
murmured something about pork chops.

Everyday after that Mother watched for the mailman and

every night when Father came home from work she looked
at the question in his eyes and shook her head.

"If thim damned Fairbanks police would git off their lazy
backsides and answer me!" he growled.

"You and your ingenious schemes!"

Mother opened the doors and raised the screened windows
but in spite of this, the house was still close. I sat on the front
stoop, drowsy from a day in the river and waiting for a
breeze to bring a breath of cool air from the Delaware.

Supper was another hour away and I was hungry. I hoped
fervently to hear the welcome cry of the Hokey Pokey Man,
who usually came along on warm weekends. Our street, on
the occasions of his appearance, would invariably swarm
with kids who popped out from doorways, alleys, backyards
and other crevices at the sound of his call. A mere two cents
was needed for a large square of hard ice cream, wrapped in
thin waxed paper. The Hokey Pokey Man sold his wares
from a red-topped open wagon, with a counter on both sides
from which he could dispense his enticing offerings. If you
so desired, he scooped a mound of shaved ice, this for a
penny, dumped it on a piece of brown paper, doused it
liberally with real fruit juices—raspberry, pineapple, lemon
... even chocolate—and you were shortly and willingly up
to your eyebrows in fruited ecstasy. On unusually hot days
it took him longer to make his way toward our street and I
felt, at that moment, tragically certain he wouldn't appear
until nightfall. So it was a toss-up between the call for supper
and perhaps, only perhaps, Heaven would intervene and send
the Hokey Pokey Man around earlier than usual.

Straining to catch the welcome *clop-clop* of his horse's
hooves, I heard Pretty Bess come into the parlor and open the
piano. She played only passably, but her voice needed only
a minimum of accompaniment and for weeks now she had
been singing one song constantly.

It annoyed Mother. "She sounds like an Edison gramophone caught in a groove," she complained.

People in the street were dressed in their Sunday best. Groups sat on front stoops, too lazy or too hot to go into their houses, and Bess' voice, clear as a bell, came through the open window.... "a little love...a little kiss..." I smiled, smug in the knowledge that *I knew* why she sang that song so much—it was the one she was going to stake her "all" on next week when she appeared in the final contest at the Orpheum in Philadelphia. I hadn't breathed a word of it. It was *our* secret. True, several times I had had to move in quickly to drown out Davey Katz when he nearly spilled the beans within earshot of my mother. Davey, I decided, had no respect for *any*thing. Hank and Nez and Moisha had remained mum.

My aunt's husky contralto could be heard up and down the street and several times people stopped to listen. A Tin Lizzie loaded with four young men dressed in blazers, wide-banded straw hats and white summer shoes, halted abruptly; the young men piled out and clustered around our window. In a little while there was quite a crowd in front of the house. The young men joined in and sang along with Pretty Bess in a rich, soft harmony. Mother came to the front door and fanned herself and smiled. Father appeared in his slippers, watched the impromptu quartet with an embarrassed grin and returned to his pipe and book. For the next half hour the street was gay with the songs of the day..."The Trolley Car Swing"..."When Irish Eyes Are Smiling"..."Dear Old Girl"...going on until Pretty Bess finally called a halt and came to the window. There was applause. The young men winked at Bess, joined in the laughter and then got in their Tin Lizzie and whizzed off...after Bess, blushing, had refused an invitation to go along for a spin.

"How nice," Mother murmured, "it's such a lovely voice you have, Bess...a true gift indeed."

Bess smiled, very mysteriously.

The letter finally arrived from Fairbanks. Thinking that I wasn't overbright (he had stated the fact forcibly more than once), Father more-or-less ignored my presence, put the kettle on the stove, brought it to a boil and experimented in opening and sealing blank envelopes. I observed all this with secret relish, thinking of the Easter egg...Father didn't know that a real expert was around! Moreover, I guessed now what this letter business was all about...I wasn't that stupid! Finally when he felt satisfied, Father steamed open the one with the Alaska postmark and while the flap was still sticky, popped in the fake letter from Uncle Mike, placed the resealed envelope on the table edge and sat on it. He noticed, for the first time, that I followed his every move.

"What in hell are ye nosin' around here fer? Go and play with the lads!"

My mother, however, was farsighted in such matters.

"Wait a minute, young man! Do you know what your father was doing?"

"Sure," I said, "he steamed open that letter and put his forgery inside."

"Forgery, is it?" Father hopped off the table with a bellow. "Now where did ye learn about *that?*"

"I know all about such things, pop..." I was about to relieve my conscience about the Easter egg punchboard but a tiny voice within urged me to desist.

"Oh, ye do now? Well, that's jist fine!" he said. "And what will they be teachin' you next I'd like to know! When I was your age, lad—"

"Just keep quiet about this," Mother said, urging me toward the door while she pushed Father back with the other hand. "Your father is doing something for Pretty Bess."

"I won't say a thing," I promised.

Mother made one of her rare phone calls that night, taking me along to Mr. Armitage, who had a wall phone in his little

office. The old man was anxious to oblige. He worked the
crank and made the connection for Mother. There was a
long wait until the party in Philadelphia located Pretty Bess.
Mother was brief:

"Mike has written to Sandy. When can you come?"

I heard the shriek on the other end.

"Yes, dear . . . Mike's well," Mother said. "Everything's
fine. He sends his love to you . . . no, he says nothing about
coming back yet. . . . What, Bess? . . . louder . . . oh . . . you'll
come down tonight? Fine . . . I said *fine*. Goodbye, dear . . .
goodbye." Mother hung up, paid Mr. Armitage and we left.

Pretty Bess lost no time in taking the trolley down from
Philadelphia. She burst into the house, hat tilted back on her
head and cheeks flushed with excitement. Father was prepared. He put on his glasses and was about to read the letter
to her when Pretty Bess grabbed it.

"Please, Sandy . . . let me."

She made little oh's and blew her nose. She sat down and
read it through again, for the third time. Father watched
her placidly. "See now, lass? Didn't I tell ye he was fine?"

"Yes. Yes . . . oh, the darling man!"

Mother observed this tableau with raised brows. Once she
looked at Father as though to imply . . . *how could you arouse
her hopes this way?*

He avoided Mother's glance and maintained his serenity.

Pretty Bess folded the letter and wiped her eyes. She was
quiet for a long time.

"D'ye feel better now, lass?" Father asked softly.

It must have been exactly the wrong thing to say. Bess
suddenly broke into sobs—loud, choking tears that made my
mother cast a look of fury at Father, then get up to console
her sister. "There, there girl . . ." Mother said. "There now!"

Abruptly, Pretty Bess wrenched away from Mother's arms
and walked to the kitchen door. Mother frowned. Father
busied himself tying an already perfectly knotted shoelace.

"I feel horrible!" Bess turned and faced us again. "I know you'll both be surer than ever that I'm self-centered and selfish and I've not an ounce of gratitude in me . . ."

"Why should we, Bess?" Mother said. "Why on earth do you say such things? All we want is your happiness . . ."

Bess bit her lips and blurted, "I was ready to leave for Alaska."

"Oh—" Mother said. "Oh my!"

It was Father's turn to throw his own scathing, superior glance—toward Mother, of course. "This here letter was jist in time, eh?"

"No, you don't understand." Faltering a little, Bess told Mother and Father about entering the Orpheum contest. Mother was sad although less concerned, I think, about the pitfalls of theatrical life than about her sister's stubborn ambition and her persistent secrecy. My father blinked in consternation. As for me, I listened raptly and waited for the dramatic finish. I held my breath and, as Pretty Bess' revelation neared its climax, I almost burst with anticipation. She spoke more and more rapidly, a bit choked; I wondered, *will she never tell us that she won the Orpheum finals?*

It came. But I was shattered.

"I lost!" Pretty Bess said. Then anger crept into her voice. "It wasn't fair . . . it wasn't fair!"

"What wasn't?" Father asked.

"That girl—the girl who won—was *trained* . . ."

"If ye'd won, ye'd jist have gone off, like that?"

"Oh . . . I would have . . . I would!"

My mother was silent and seemed to find no word of comfort to offer Bess. My aunt bowed her head and wept anew for her disappointment and her hurt, for the injustice done her. Then Mother said quietly, "I read in the *Gazette* that this girl comes from the most poverty-stricken lot in south Philly—a half-orphan, if I remember it—and the nuns at the school pinched together money for her lessons."

Bess sniffed. Father stroked her hand.

"And it took a lot of years and a lot of hard work to get up there finally on the stage.

Bess swallowed. "Well?"

"I'm asking you," Mother said.

"I knew in my bones she was no amateur—" Bess stopped. Her eyes flashed suddenly and her voice became animated as the words rolled out. "I'm being unfair, I guess. All right. All right, I admit it! She sang wonderfully, sis . . . beautifully . . . you should have heard her. She deserved to win! I'm glad she got it and I'm even glad I lost. . . ."

"I believe the lass, Lady," Father said. "Look at her face."

Bess rushed over to hug Mother. "If there's any running off that Bess O'Hara does, it'll be running off every week for that voice training . . ."

Now Mother got weepy and Father blew his nose although he had no sign of a cold. I watched the affair with an ominous frown.

"I'm glad I lost," Pretty Bess repeated, even defiantly, it seemed, "because when it was all over and I walked out I felt terribly sorry for myself. And I thought there'd be nothing to look forward to, and the bottom dropped out of everything. Then I said: 'Bess O'Hara, you're forgetting something in this self-pity.' And I thought, and I remembered what it was. If I had won, I'd have lost my own family!" She giggled. "I'm no half-orphan, sis . . . and what's more, I've no intention to become a part-time relative either!"

"B'jesus!" Father said. "That's the stuff, girl!"

I started out the door. I knew how Bess felt because I remembered, too—how I had left home and how happy I had been to wake up again in my own bed. Life was becoming just too darned complicated. If only Uncle Mike would come back. I needed him, for after all, he was a man of the world!

CHAPTER X

Throw Him Down McCloskey

Throw him down McCloskey
Was to be the battle cry,
Throw him down McCloskey
You can lick him if you try . . .
And future generations
With wonder and delight
Will read on history's pages
Of the great McCloskey fight.

WHEN OUR STREET was dug up and sewers were laid, and the old wooden biffys in the rear of the houses dismantled and replaced by indoor affairs, everyone was excited, to be sure. For those who had difficulty in adapting, it meant that a Board of Health officer had to visit the newly arrived immigrant families and explain that the square enamel contraption with the enclosed copper balls was *not* an ideal place to keep a live carp until it was ready for the stove. It also heralded the end of those antiquated under-the-bed affairs referred to politely in our house as "chambers," and by our next-door neighbors the Katzes as "pishteppels."

Be all that as it may, the extinction and replacement of the outdoor biffys was to become memorable, not because it indicated an onward-and-upward cultural trend, but for another reason entirely.

For one whole month our street had been a delightful mess: a great deep trench ran down the center, and piled on top of the excavated dirt were enchanting concrete sewer pipe sections, each large enough in diameter to crawl into with ease. The oldsters, of course, complained, and on rainy days they became sullen and uncommunicative, for mud tracks abounded indoors and out.

Old Man Knowles got drunk of a Saturday night and fell into the trench. He sat in the yellow mud up to his chin until Mrs. Knowles went looking for him and caught a glint of his eyes and nose protruding from the goo. She hooted plaintively for assistance and in short order the neighbors had hauled out Mr. Knowles (who resembled a happy stoat after a mud bath) and carried him to the rear of his house, where my father hooked up a hose and washed him off, clothes and all, while Mr. Knowles stood erect in a galvanized tub and crooned "Rock of Ages." That, it seemed, was the only melody Mr. Knowles ever mastered.

But all things have to end, and the day came when the city laborers finished the job. The street was repaved, the biffys in the backyards were gone and in each house now was a gleaming white affair in a small cubbyhole referred to as the "bathroom," although bathtubs were not among the installations. They came later.

The Katzes were agog with the new gadget. Through our connecting wall we could hear hysterical arguments between Mr. and Mrs. Katz, and an occasional wallop aimed at either Davey or Moisha, who were having a great time flushing things down the drain, including all of Uncle Jake's spare socks. The next day Mr. Katz, as usual, brought his junk wagon to the house at noon and was immediately enlisted by his wife in the task of releasing Davey's left foot from the bowl, where it was caught tightly after he had experimented in a new and novel way of washing feet with minimum effort. Davey was howling blue murder when Mr. Katz came upon the scene. His first and natural reaction was to clout Davey, perhaps instinctively realizing that he would never again find his offspring in a position wherein he couldn't duck or run. Mr. Katz, too, was in desperate need of some sort of outlet for his own pain and frustration, for all that morning he had made his rounds with a mouth full of new false teeth purchased at great expense. He was, therefore, only too happy to clout Davey a few when he found him trapped.

Anyhow, after much shouting and wailing, Mr. Katz uncorked Davey, counted the toes to see if they were intact and then leaned over to see just what *did* happen when someone pulled the flush chain. At that instant, perhaps from the exertion of unplugging his son, Mr. Katz hiccupped. His teeth popped out...and down the drain. There was an ominous long silence as Mr. and Mrs. Katz stared at each other...and then they both let loose. Mr. Katz began to bellow and tried to rip the bowl off its base while Mrs. Katz built a sirenlike wail that all but peeled the wallpaper off every house on the block as it penetrated slowly but insistently. I was in our backyard at the moment and wondered if the siren noise was from across the river in New Jersey...they sometimes blew such whistles over there when fire broke out.

Mother came to the back stoop. "What's that strange noise?" she asked no one in particular.

Father had just come home from the job, and he too looked out. After a moment he declared, "It's right next door. Them poor Katzes. Somebody's probably passed away!"

Mother gasped and started around the alley toward the Katz backyard. Father followed, looking very solemn. "Them furriners, the Hebrews," he said, "have a special kind o' keenin'...almost like the Old Country." That, of course, meant Ireland. To my father there was no other nation overseas except Ireland...and it took several years of patient schooling by teachers in our town of Chester to convince me otherwise.

I went along at a safe distance, knowing my old man would boot me if I followed too closely. However, others had heard the noise and several of the neighbors had made a beeline for the Katzes' simultaneously.

"Some poor soul's gone to its Maker fer sure," Father said, shaking his head. For the wailing came from upstairs, and in those days anything that happened upstairs in daylight hours —in our circles, at least—carried morbid connotations: either someone was seriously ill, and was therefore in bed, or some character had given up the spirit. Otherwise bedrooms were for sleeping—at night.

Davey met the neighbors at the foot of the stairs.

"It's pop," he announced to all in general.

"Poor man," said Father. "Whin did it happen?"

"It only just begun," Davey said, and stalked off.

A moment later mass disillusionment set in when the neighbors found Mr. Katz very much alive and Mrs. Katz now at a new peak and desperately trying to pull her husband's entire arm out of the drain. In a jiffy Father and Mr. Knowles (who had showed up humming his favorite tune, but sober) had Mr. Katz unlatched, on his feet and emitting strange *phoophing* noises because of the absence of teeth. He also kept trying to get his hand down the drain again. Father and Mr. Knowles restrained him, Mr. Knowles eventually placing a firm hammerlock on the small, skinny junkman.

Perhaps a full hour lapsed before the nature and enormity of the loss became fully established.

"Well," said Father, "T'aint the end of the world. We'll jist use our mechanical ingenuity and retrieve the lost item."

Mr. Knowles nodded and hummed to himself. The women clucked sympathetically over Mrs. Katz, while that poor woman sobbed and tried to get everybody to sit down to tea. Mr. Knowles then disappeared but quickly reappeared smelling of strong schnapps, perhaps from Uncle Jake's private stores in the cellar. Anyhow, he hummed louder than before and his sleeves were now rolled up for action.

Well, up until almost midnight Father and Mr. Knowles contrived, calculated, constructed doohickeys and gadgets with which they probed to snag the missing dentures. To no avail. Uncle Jake had come home and immediately barricaded himself in the cellar, perhaps realizing that his precious store of schnapps was in danger with Mr. Knowles in near proximity.

Sometime during the late hours Father and Mr. Knowles decided on broader and more drastic tactics. They turned off the water and dismantled the whole shebang. Mr. Katz seemed to have gone into a coma. His wife moistened his pale forehead occasionally with wet towels, but he showed no interest in activities around him. Mother got us to bed and hauled Father home shortly after midnight. Mr. Knowles repaired to Murphy's saloon.

Early the following day Mr. Katz, his mouth firm if ever so puckered, was seen fussing about the front of the house armed with a pickax, several shovels and a red lantern that he lit and placed on the sidewalk despite the bright morning sun. Apparently he thought one wasn't permitted to dig up a thoroughfare without a lighted red lantern, whereas *with* one, one could.

A half hour later, with Mr. Katz three feet deep in the sidewalk, a policeman appeared.

"Now git outa that hole, man! Ye can't go around disturbin' the public right-of-way in that fashion!"

Mr. Katz spoke no English, but he glared up at the policeman with a fiendish obstinacy. The policeman sighed, reached down and hauled Mr. Katz out of the hole. Mr. Katz at once hit him with the pick handle. Mrs. Katz appeared at the front door and once again slowly ascended the wailing scale until every woman on the street, plus a few night-worker males, turned out in mass.

Mr. Knowles, it seemed, had overstayed at Murphy's and hadn't gone to work that morning. He came to the front stoop, yawning, and in a sour mood. His eyes lit up when he saw the little junkman in the firm grasp of the law. Mr. Knowles casually walked over to the policeman and slugged him. The policeman sighed again, released Mr. Katz and promptly lost consciousness. Mrs. Katz reached a *new* note, surpassing that attained the night before.

The policeman, quickly aroused to consciousness by the increasing bedlam, sat up, stood up, reached down, pulled up Mr. Katz out of the hole, then turned and grabbed Mr. Knowles as well. Whereupon both Mr. Katz and Mr. Knowles proceeded to beat upon the policeman. Mrs. Katz

tried to pull her husband away just as the policeman un-
limbered his nightstick and swung. The heavy wooden ap-
peaser missed Mr. Knowles but landed on Mrs. Katz's head,
which was topped by a thick bun. She sat on the sidewalk,
noteless, as Mr. Knowles swung a haymaker, missed, and fell
headlong into the hole.

A few minutes later Mr. Katz and his defender were hand-
cuffed and marched off to the local jail just three blocks
away. My mother and several neighboring women spent the
balance of the day with Mrs. Katz assuring the bereft lady
that things would be set right when my father and the rest
of the neighborhood menfolk came home from work. But
along about three o'clock that afternoon Magistrate Flaherty
and Police Chief McCluskey showed up. The judge, like
everybody from the mayor down, was running for reelection.
The two men stood quietly looking into the shallow hole in
front of the Katz house, oblivious to the frowning womenfolk who eyed them from nearby windows.

"So this's the scene o' the crime!" Magistrate Flaherty
said. He stared hard at Police Chief McCluskey.

"Well, the man was apprehended in th' commission of a
felony!" the Chief said.

"A misdemeanor at the very most."

"The accused was committin' a public nuisance, endan-
gerin' the lives of decent law abidin' citizens."

"Officer Peters used brutal force on this poor furriner. He
also arrested a hero of Ninety-eight!" (Actually Mr. Knowles
was dishonorably discharged from the Rough Riders when
he packed up and went AWOL declaring, as it later came
out in his court-martial, "T'hell with it, men!" A sentiment
and phrase he was to pass on, as I've mentioned, to his son
Nez. He also did a year in a Philippine army stockade.)

The two city guardians finally left the scene, but within
the hour Mr. Katz's puny excavating efforts were put to
shame by the herculean heft of a city-laborer gang that began

immediately tearing up the sidewalk and street in search of the main sewer piping only recently installed. My mother raised the parlor window of the Katz house and demanded to know what in the world did those men think they were doing?

A big man, probably the foreman (for he was sitting on the Katz stone doorstep) said: "Madame, I have in me possession a court order to proceed (he squinted at a folded piece of paper) *forthwith!*"

"Forwith *what?*" my mother said in her crispest tone. That stumped the foreman.

"All I know, lady, is Judge Flaherty says find them goddam teeth!"

My mother couldn't oppose even the remotest chance of retrieving the Katz choppers, so she glanced skyward and frowned (it was clouding up) and muttered something about "more mud again" and closed the window.

At five o'clock my father came home and was soon joined by other menfolk who all watched the diggers with professional, if jaundiced, eyes, occasionally commenting in derogatory terms about the slovenliness and incompetence of city laborers.

The diggers had just reached the top of the main sewer line when the bell of a paddy wagon was heard at the head of our street. It was followed by a second paddy wagon, loaded with policemen. Chief McCluskey climbed out of the first wagon and stalked over to the now very deep ditch. It had just started to rain, and while the chief was ordering the laborers out of the big ditch, saying he didn't give a damn about any court order because the judge was looking for votes, not lost dentures, and the judge might fool some of the people some of the time and so on. Anyhow, my father told the chief he was a heartless man and he'd better take his minions out of the neighborhood instantly, whereupon the chief ordered my father to depart quietly or join Mr. Katz and Mr. Knowles in the local pokey. My father turned bright red and started to roll up his sleeves. At that point two policemen grabbed him, and as they did the neighborhood menfolk *and* the ditchdiggers were suddenly a noisy, swirling, slugging, soggy mass of punches, picks, clubs and fists flying every which way. The womenfolk now came on the scene quickly, the rain began in torrential earnestness, and bodies were plopping into the muddy ditch and bouncing back into the fray.

All came to a grinding halt when the cops, the panting laborers and the neighborhood menfolk saw an unbelievable sight emerge out of the driving rain. First came the color guard: three soggy flags carried by three aging troopers, the stars and stripes in the center, carried by Judge Flaherty—a uniformed trooper with the flag of the 102nd Pennsys—the third banner that of the county. Behind them marched a company of the local National Guard.

The judge bellowed the command to halt. Chief McCluskey stared speechless, his big nose bleeding.

"In the name of National security," the judge proclaimed, "you are hereby ordered to retire to your place of business or your legal domicile forthwith!"

The crowd, including my father (who also had a bleeding nose) was impressed.

The police chief found his voice. "Ya got no right to bring armed troops into a peaceful citizens' gatherin'—"

"T'hell I ain't," the judge shouted. "We was jist musterin' over at the armory for weekly trainin' whin we got word that your cops was beatin' honest laborers and peaceful voters— ah—peaceful *citizens!*"

The argument went on for another several tense moments and the guardsmen, stiffly in formation, looking menacing. My father walked over to the judge and the two men conversed quietly for a short spell. Finally the judge beckoned Chief McCluskey over and the three talked a while.

The upshot was a great letdown for the National Guard, for total peace was declared then and there.

Judge Flaherty raised his voice for the whole neighborhood to hear. "Before I again order you all to disperse, I have an announcement." He turned to the rigid guardsmen. "Corporal Hennings, front an' center!"

A stocky trooper stepped forward.

"Corporal, you made Mr. Katz false teeth, right?"

"Yes, Captain Flaherty," the corporal agreed. "I'm the county dentist." (Mr. Katz hadn't been able to pay the full tab on his dentures.)

"How much did Mr. Katz's bill come to?" the judge asked.

"Well, captain, it was pretty steep—twenty-seven dollars!"

During the next ten minutes thirty dollars was collected in Chief McCluskey's soggy helmet. My father gave a whole dollar. Then the chief announced that the ditch would be immediately filled in and Mr. Katz and Mr. Knowles would be home in time for supper.

That night my mother asked Father what brought about the sudden cessation of hostilities.

"I jist convinced the judge and Chief McCluskey that when the paper spread the news of their joint humanitarian efforts —they both would benefit. . . ."

"But how in the world . . ." my mother began, quite puzzled.

"It's men's business," my father said smugly. "Also, ye can perform miracles around election time."

CHAPTER XI

Give Me That Old Time Religion

Give me that old time religion,
Give me that old time religion,
Give me that old time religion,
It's good enough for me.

It was good for the Hebrew children,
It was good for the Hebrew children,
It was good for the Hebrew children,
It's good enough for me.

To THIS VERY DAY I am convinced that my friend Nez Knowles and I were directly instrumental in bringing about the redemption of a fallen woman, although the grown-ups of our neighborhood believed she was saved by a visiting evangelist.

Miss Louella, the fallen woman in question, was a tall, thinnish old maid who, as I've said, earned her living as sort of a journeyman seamstress, and while our mothers of necessity were adept with needle and thread, Miss Louella, it seemed, was an uncanny needle-plier in two respects: she could make strong neat buttonholes in old garments, and she could create out of odds and ends a side-split peg skirt, a mode very much favored by the ladies of the day. It was also common knowledge, however, as for example she'd demonstrated at my Uncle Mike's going-away party, that Miss Louella was fond of copious draughts of strong, blackish porter, a kind of ale with hair on its chest. There was, to be sure, a bit of drinking in a rough-and-tumble neighborhood like ours, but it was confined almost exclusively to the men-folk, who were rarely seen in their cups publicly. For a lady to take more than an infrequent nip on gala occasions such as weddings or wakes was unthinkable. Miss Louella, there-fore, was generally referred to in whispered conversation among the women as the "poor dear" of the "isn't it a shame" department.

Miss Louella lived alone in a two-room flat over a feedstore up at the end of our street. Our mothers knew very little of her background, for Miss Louella carefully confined her

conversation to the present tense, and then generally to current styles or materials and the state of her health, the latter
subject a convenient ruse to account for her known addiction
to porter, which she declared she simply had to take, being so
advised by her doctor, to combat frequent spells of "malaise."
No one knew her doctor, nor did she ever name him. But
everyone knew the saloon across the street from the feedstore
where Miss Louella, of evenings, flitted in and out the side
door marked "Family Entrance" with a large tin growler
carefully hidden inside a birdcage she kept covered with a
beautiful rose-patterned hood.

On these trips to and from the saloon Miss Louella extended the birdcage delicately in front of her, with one hand,
as a person might do in transporting a live bird. Occasionally
she would whistle little bird notes. In spite of Miss Louella's
fondness for porter, however, the women of the neighborhood believed, with a kind of feminine intuition, that somehow, somewhere, she had been a *lady*, for she kept strictly to
herself, never used unladylike expressions, was neat as a pin
and always had a kind word to say about her customers. Remarkably, she didn't gossip.

Miss Louella, however, had begun to imbibe more frequently, and on several occasions she had turned up at customers' houses in rather sorry shape. I recall Mother saying
to my father, "The poor dear woman is beginning to make a
spectacle of herself," and Father remarking that "there ought
to be a law against saloons dispensing alcoholic beverages
to females from side entrances."

It was also around this time that Mother decided to make
it her business to learn what religion, if any, Miss Louella adhered to; her idea seemed to be to ring a Man of the Cloth
into the deal, and when Miss Louella showed up a few days
later to finish the seams on Aunt Bess' green satin dress,
Mother went to work on the old girl. I was in the kitchen
pestering the cat, being confined to quarters that warm day

because of a sore throat. Miss Louella placed her big carpet-bag on the table and smiled at me in a sort of blurred way. Mother put two cups on the table, poured hot water from the teakettle which was always on the stove, and after admonishing me to let the poor helpless cat alone or she'd break my neck, began to chat with Miss Louella.

Mother opened the conversation obliquely, remarking upon the sudden appearance of large placards in town heralding the imminent arrival of Billy Sunday. Even I knew who Billy Sunday was—it was said he had saved more souls than anyone since St. Martin himself, Patron Saint of Innkeepers and Drunkards, who shared his coat with a beggar. Miss Louella sat primly on the edge of her chair, sipped her tea and smiled at Mother. Her straight thin frame was, despite the warm weather, encased in a black silk dress; she wore high black shoes with glass buttons and a bonnet that was as much a part of her as the big sewing bag. The hat was a tiny black straw upon which sprouted a single, rigid white feather that stood erect and hooked forward at the tip, somewhat like the feeler on a beetle.

"I've heard so much about the man," Mother said, referring to Mr. Billy Sunday, "I wonder what his faith might be?"

Miss Louella shook her head from side to side and continued to smile vaguely.

"Do you think, now, he might be one of these here Methodists?" Mother pursued, determined to get Miss Louella involved in an ecclesiastical dialogue. Miss Louella sighed deeply, exhaled, and I caught a strong pungent odor of porter all the way across the kitchen. Albert sniffed and flattened his ears.

"I don't know what his faith is, Mrs. Mullen," Miss Louella finally said. Mother beamed and her expression was one of waiting for more. "The good man," Miss Louella murmured, "certainly has helped a lot of people to a better way of life."

Mother brightened. She sensed an opening and moved in

swiftly. "Yes, indeed! And *so* many people need to be helped in these trying times!"

Miss Louella nodded.

"And the pity is," Mother went on quickly, "*so* many fall into a sorry way of life without *meaning* to!" She looked pointedly at Miss Louella but that lady merely nodded sympathetically. She exhaled another enormous sigh and Mother, within immediate range, winced. She hurried over to the window, halted before it and remarked in feigned surprise, "My goodness, the window *is* open."

Mother, a determined woman, finally got to the point. "And what might your church be, Miss Louella? Not, mind you, that I'm one to be nosey."

Miss Louella smiled. "Oh, I don't think you're being nosey at all, Mrs. Mullen."

Mother waited for more, but the old lady busied herself with her big sewing bag and said no more. That seemed to end the matter.

The next day Mother felt my head, peered down my throat and pronounced me fit to depart and get out from under her feet. I hurried out into the alley, searched the wind and ground for clues as to the whereabouts of my colleagues. I scaled up the high alley fence, balanced like a tightrope walker, and saw that my gang was not at the moment engaged in any of its usual pursuits, like hiding up in the thick foliaged chestnut trees in the Quaker Church yard, nor was there any sight of them on the prowl around the equally forbidden territory in the rear of the Pickle Works, nor did I see any flitting forms on the sloped roof of the livery stables next to the Quaker Church. And I knew, without having to consult an almanac, the precise state of the tide in the nearby river; it was dead low at that hour of that particular day, so the gang certainly wasn't swimming. I sat on top of the fence and tried to figure out where everyone might be. It was possible though not probable they might have gone off—Nez,

Hank and Moisha, the older, in the lead, and Frank and Davey following in the rear—loaded down with nice round stones (as sort of an ammunition supply train) in a hit-and-run raid on the Potter Street Pugs. But I ruled that out, for stone fights mostly took place right before sundown, this giving the defeated side a chance to run like hell until covered by darkness, and it was now too early in the day.

I got down off the fence and wandered disconsolately out into the street, where I saw Hank's little sister Mamie and commanded her to halt. Under my prodding Mamie lisped the information that my gang was over on the Fair lot. "Ith's a thircuth," she said. Now the circus had come and gone a month earlier so I knew something else cooked over on the lot. I dismissed Mamie with a curt nod and she went her barefoot way. Ten minutes later I was with my friends. It was a beautiful sight. Men were busy erecting the biggest tent I'd ever seen outside the annual visit of the Sells-Floto Circus. Thousands of collapsible wooden chairs were being unloaded from horse-drawn wagons and several advance men stood around directing the work. Hank, Nez and Moisha were red-faced from happy exertion, staggering off with batches of chairs handed down by men on the wagons. A few of the Potter Street Pugs were similarly engaged. In times like these, when there was a bonanza dime or quarter to be earned, hostilities were held in abeyance. Hank pointed to a man and I went to him and offered my services. He was a plump, bald individual, chewing gum. He looked me over. "Well, son, it's right nice of you to volunteer your services to The Lord. He'll sure reward you." He smiled in a fatherly manner.

"How much?" I asked.

He dropped his fatherly air. "Two bits when you finish."

I joined my gang, unloading the chairs. We earned our two bits indeed. I never saw so many chairs in my life. But just the opportunity to stagger with them into the vast, awesome

interior of the tent was worth it. Workmen hammered together a wide wooden platform up front while others sweated
and strained a huge, battered pump organ into place. Billy
Sunday sure did everything in a big way. Eventually when
we had finished our backbreaking chore and each had received twenty-five cents, we were told if we turned up
bright and early Saturday morning to distribute handbills we
would get another quarter. That suited us fine, so we took
off and headed for Schiller's Ice Cream Parlor. We were,
collectively, stinking rich. An hour later, we were, individually, stinking sick. We went home.

The next day was routine. Moisha got stepped on by a
dray horse while we played follow-the-leader under various
horses' bellies, the horses being lined up as wagons loaded
at the big produce market at the other end of our street;
Hank tore his brand new corduroy pants as we made a
getaway over the fence behind the wholesale banana market;
and I sustained a head nick that required only an adhesive
patch when we accidentally ran into a marauding party of
the Potter Street Pugs.

That night after supper we met in our back alley and discussed ways and means of enjoying the soft, hazy night. None
of us had any new ideas, so we decided to play Hats Off.
It was a simple game and required only a long strong piece of
black or dark gray thread. Moisha had dreamed it up during
one of his frequent somber moods. Nez ran home and returned with the necessary thread. We went up to the corner.
Our base of operation for Hats Off was the feedstore under
Miss Louella's flat. There was a telephone pole directly in
front of the store, and stacked up against the outer wall of
the place were dozens of large bags of feed. We tied one end
of the dark thread to the pole, about five and a half feet high,
then climbed up on the feed bags which were piled about
five feet high and protected by a canvas awning overhead.
There was a lone, very dim streetlamp across the way in

front of the saloon, so we were nicely hidden from passersby. In this fashion we stretched the invisible thread across the sidewalk, to make a kind of a hand-maneuvered horizontal trap.

Now, every grown male in those days wore either a hat or a cap, and this being summer, straw hats were in abundance. When occupied in this endeavor, we had to remain absolutely quiet, no matter how ridiculous our suspecting victims acted. Our first customers that night were two men who wore bright-banded straw hats. I maneuvered the taut thread, and I knew from much experience you had to nail the *tallest* of any two people who came along, providing they were walking together.

As the two men walked under the thread, I dumped the tall man's hat. As was always the case, the victim halted in midstride, uttered an exclamation of surprise, puzzled by an unseen hand gently brushing his hat from his head. The shorter man picked up the hat for him, vowed *he* had *not* been playing tricks. I let them go on their way. It was an operation that required an intuitive sense about the intelligence and character of the victim, and I felt once was enough for this individual. He struck me as being pretty smart, which meant enough was enough. Moisha, the originator of Hats Off, held the world record at this time, having successfully dumped the chapeau of one gentleman four times running on the same night. The laws of physics, being what they are, always dumped a hat *behind* the stride of the victim, so that when he took a few steps to the rear to retrieve it and started forward again it was a simple matter to repeat the process if one so desired, or dared.

Our next customer that night was Nez Knowles' own father. Nez whispered fiercely to me to lay off as his father approached, knowing his old man would whale hell out of him should he discover us, but I believed in playing no favorites. Anyhow, I was, so to speak, in the driver's seat. His father wore a black derby in all seasons, and one had to be real expert with the thread to dump a derby, due to the smooth, firm curve of the crown. (Because of its rough texture you could dump a straw hat so long as you caught the crown anywhere above the brim.) I caught Mr. Knowles' derby with a deft aim, and it toppled to the sidewalk. I was aware of Mr. Knowles' evil temper, but even I was startled at the blasphemous stream he uttered as he glared about him, suspecting probably some hidden culprit across the street with a slingshot or beanshooter. I felt Nez's fingernails in my leg in silent entreaty to lay off, so I let Mr. Knowles go his way, muttering loudly to himself.

Seeing there were no new victims on the horizon, I turned the thread over to Nez, feeling perhaps that I owed him some gesture after what I'd done to his flesh and blood. Nez was angry when he took the thread and I suppose that accounted for what happened next. He was so mad at me that he deliberately violated the ground rules of the game, which were, to wit, *never* dump a lady's hat. I lay back against the wall, surfeited at the moment, while Nez, Moisha, Davey and Frank peered in both directions up and down the sidewalk.

If I had held the thread, it certainly wouldn't have happened, but then again, in the final analysis, perhaps Miss Louella wouldn't have been saved. Anyhow, Nez spied Miss Louella coming out of the Family Entrance of the saloon across the street with her covered birdcage. When she got to our side and started to pass the thread, Nez hooked it into the loop of the feather on her hat. Instead of falling to the pavement as all male headwear did, her bonnet remained magically suspended in midair. Nez joggled the thread in an attempt to drop the hat, but it only danced in a slow, hypnotic rhythm as Miss Louella stared at it, frozen to complete immobility. From habit, she still held the birdcage in front of her, but her mouth was wide open. Finally she gathered her wits and with her free hand, which shook badly, reached toward her airborne bonnet. As Nez slowly lowered the hat Miss Louella snatched her hand back and let loose with a piercing scream. She rushed to the curb, extracted the pail of porter from within the birdcage and deliberately poured the dark beverage into the gutter. She then hurried off, glancing back once at her bonnet still doing a slow dance in midair.

I saw my father emerge into the glare of the streetlight and watch curiously after the rapidly disappearing spinster. I muttered a warning to my colleagues. My father came abreast of the bonnet and stared at it. I held my breath. He scratched his chin and gazed around. He reached up and held the bonnet. Then his eyes turned to where we were hiding up on the feed sacks in the dark. He said nothing at all. He deliberately felt for the thread and found it. With one quick yank he snapped it. Then he took the bonnet to the nearby telephone pole and hung it on a nail or tack that held a placard ad. To our surprise he whistled to himself as he walked off.

I sighed in relief and turned on Nez. "You crazy nut! You went and broke the rules."

Nez merely replied, "T' hell with it, men," and climbed down and went off somewhere. When I got home I lost no time in scooting upstairs to bed, my father watching me, tongue in cheek, the way he often did when he was thinking hard about something. He didn't say a word.

The following morning we turned up at the revival tent and were given armloads of handbills to distribute. There was enough to keep us busy, had we so chosen, for the next several hours, but we had from time to time previously hired out for similar jobs, so we spent the next fifteen minutes faithfully shoving handbills under doors in the immediate vicinity of the Fair lot, and as soon as we were far enough away deposited the balance down the nearest sewer. We returned to the Fair lot for about an hour before the big evangelical gathering aimed at cleansing the town of sin was due to start and found the tent was already full of people. We received our twenty-five cents, after swearing solemnly we had distributed every one, then we entered the tent to be saved too and found ourselves choice seats up front.

Billy Sunday's organist was rendering "Give Me That Old Time Religion" ... and sundry other soul-shaking numbers, and the huge crowd had joined in singing before Billy Sunday himself finally strode with buoyant, bouncing steps onto the platform, to be greeted with an earsplitting welcome. We younger members of the throng got into the mood of the thing quickly and easily, chirping repeated hallelujahs along with our elders and clapping our hands in swaying unison as Mr. Sunday gradually stepped up the pace of his full-voiced incantations.

I was thrilled when he demonstrated his contempt for Lucifer by taking the stance of a home run hitter at bat, each time delivering a terrific wallop, or winding up like a big league pitcher and striking out the devil with finesse. Having had considerable sandlot experience myself, I recognized big-time stuff when I saw it.

When Mr. Sunday came to that awaited part of his sermon, preluded by soft organ music, and asked who would be the first to walk up that sawdust covered trail to the platform and confess his sins, I felt my skin prickle. It was hypnotic. We joined the great crowd in falling silent and craning our necks to witness the emergence of the first courageous sinner. It didn't take long. Somewhere in the rear a man shouted, "I'm coming, Lord!" and he marched right up the aisle. The crowd went wild. Then the sinners popped out from everywhere, including a surprising number of elderly men and women who tottered down the aisle with tear-stained faces. In short order Mr. Sunday was confronted with enough wrongdoers to tax the strength of St. Peter himself, but he went about it manfully. The big tent quivered with the vibrations of screaming witnesses (those still remaining seated and

180 In a Year of Our Lord

apparently deficient in sin) who encouraged the acknowl-
edged fallen souls to "you-tell-it-all-and-don't-be-afeerd."

Mr. Sunday went on his knees on the platform, and the
sawdust aisle was empty to lost souls when, suddenly, the last
sinner appeared. It was Miss Louella. Hatless. I saw her face
as she moved by, the picture of saintliness. She walked with
dignity, her tall skinny form unhurried, her eyes shining
with a beautiful expression of peace.

Weeks went by and I had forgotten Miss Louella. Mother
was pouring everyone some of her tangy homemade root beer
when she brought up the subject.

"That woman is like a new person," she said proudly to
Father. He mumbled and continued to read but Mother went
right on. "I don't hold with these here evangelists..." she
paused thoughtfully "...but it seems they *do* accomplish
miracles once in a while, don't you agree Sandy?"

Father glanced at me and nodded. "Hmm! I suppose so!"

Obviously Mother felt she had helped Mr. Sunday move
Miss Louella in the direction of the Lord.

"The dear woman has not..." she looked at me and
frowned "...well, I must say she confines herself to tea
now." She sighed. "The ways of the Almighty..."

Father directed another look in my direction. "Yes," he said
softly, "the ways of the Lord are inscrutable, indeed."

CHAPTER XII

Just a Little Lovin'
for Baby, Please

Honey dear, where you bin?
Glad you're here . . . Come on in . . .
Creep up near
Taint no sin,
If we're going to do some lovin'
Let's begin,
Honey dove, I've been sad . . .
Need some love,
Need it bad . . .

LIKE MOST SMALL TOWNS in the young 1900's Chester had the usual by-products of adult frustration in the form of a Watch & Ward Society and a more vociferous group called Against Sin & Shame. The latter was in operation only a short time before the townfolk began referring to it by its initials— but by then the ladies who formed the organization had invested a considerable sum in letterheads and had incorporated the name . . . so it was too late.

One day we—that is, Davey, Moisha, Frank and I—got mixed up with the reformers accidently when we were chased back to our neighborhood by the Potter Street Pugs. As we puffed along with the Pugs breathing down our necks, we halted abruptly, because dashing toward us from the other end of the street was the horse-drawn paddy wagon loaded with cops. Some unkind soul had turned them loose on us. The Pugs evaporated like wraiths. We had no alternative but to dash between two of the nearest houses, plunge over a back fence, through more labyrinths, more streets, the shouts of our pursuers painfully loud. Then—a miracle! A beautiful lady appeared at a back door and beckoned us into her kitchen. I say "beautiful," because she was just that, even to *our* age group—a golden complexion, cherry-red lips, great black eyes that sparkled like pitch in the sun. She shut the door and shoved us under the kitchen table. A fist pounded the door. She opened it.

"You gentlemen wish to come in?" she purred sweetly.

"Not this trip, sis," one of the policemen said. "You seen a bunch of little bastards go by here?"

"All sorts come and go," she said. "Just what is the trouble, Mr. DeMain?" She seemed to know the policeman.

"It's those Graham and Potter Street kids. Heavin' rocks at each other and disturbin' the peace."

We heard a throaty chuckle. "Boys will be boys!" The door closed, the tablecloth lifted. "You little bastards can come out now."

We stood erect, awed at this tall lady who smelled so good.

"What would you like first...chocolate cake or ice cream?"

We were struck inarticulate at the very idea. Davey was more sophisticated.

"What flavor ice cream?" he demanded.

She ruffled his hair. "Who's your daddy?"

"The junkman," Davey said. "Strawberry?"

"Vanilla. There are two junkmen. Which one's your daddy?"

"The other one," Davey said. "How about peach?"

"Only vanilla. Now sit down while I dish it out."

So for the next fifteen minutes we gorged on our unexpected manna while the beautiful lady sat and thoughtfully watched us, her red lips compressed. She occasionally nodded as though quietly debating with herself.

"How would you all like to earn a quarter?" she finally asked.

This was simply *too* good. First she saves us from the Law, then satiates us with cake and ice cream...now she offers us the staggering sum of twenty-five cents each.

It was Davey again who initiated the dialogue.

"It's worth thirty cents," he said flatly.

"What's worth thirty cents?" Frank asked, bug-eyed with confusion.

Davey held his ground, waiting for market developments. The dusky lady narrowed her big eyes at our negotiator. "Yeah...what's worth thirty cents, little man?"

"Okay, we'll take a quarter," Davey said with a tone of finality.

"What's ... what's ..." This was as far as Moisha got.

"I want you boys to play a game with me," the lady said mysteriously.

Well now, we were always ready for games. ...

"Some people will be here soon," she went on, "and I want to play a joke on them."

This sounded swell. We all perked up. Who knew? This could lead to another round of cake and ice cream too.

"What kinda game?" Davey demanded. He looked around inquiringly. There were none of the usual accoutrements, no clubs, hockey sticks, mitts, slingshots or rocks.

"There will be some nice ladies here in a few minutes. I want you boys to call me Mother when they get here."

"I *got* a Mother," Frank objected.

"But this is only a *game* ... just fooling, kind of." She smiled.

We were tempted, but puzzled.

"All right—thirty cents!" she said quickly.

"Sold!" Davey snapped.

She smiled and tapped us each on the head.

"Let's see ... John ... James ... Jerry ... and Jesse."

Davey was the last knighted. "That's me ... Jesse James!" he shouted.

"You'll make it someday," the beautiful lady commented.

A knock sounded at the back door. The lady frowned. "They can't be coming in the *back* way." She opened the door and revealed a man blinking in the sun.

" 'Scuse me. Is Goldie in?" he asked politely.

"I'm Goldie. Beat it, Fred."

"Geez, I din't recognize ya with yer duds on." Fred left. Goldie shut the door.

A minute later the front doorbell rang. "*That's* them." She looked very severe. "Now remember! Call me Mother! And anything I say, just look at me the way you look at your mother . . ."

She hurried to the front door and came back with three well-dressed ladies who looked pained and very pale.

"*Who* are these *youngsters?*" one demanded immediately.

"Why, my children, of course!"

Goldie beamed at us. We smiled, trying hard to look at her with the same expressions we aimed at our mothers. Except that wasn't easy, because I for one suddenly realized that most looks I directed at *my* mother weren't exactly what the lady probably had in mind . . . usually my face showed alarm (as in preparing to duck a wallop), or righteous innocence (as in preparation to telling a whopper).

In any case, the visitors seemed to view *us* with strong suspicion.

"*Your* children?" one visitor—the one with the veil over what seemed to be a cement mask—asked almost pleadingly, as though to imply *say it isn't so!*

"That's right," Goldie said. "My very own."

"But," gasped another, "they're white!" She leaned for a closer look at Moisha and Davey . . . both were pretty dark to begin with, being Jews of Romanian background, and looked more like sunburned gypsies, or so I'd once heard Nez's mother say.

"Well, they're white all right," Goldie said indulgently, "white with a teeny touch of me."

The visitors seemed to have difficulty in breathing. Goldie was all smiles. So were we. There was a big stake in this for us.

"I suppose," Goldie went on, "*you* can tell who their fathers are."

The violent breathing stopped abruptly, as though somebody had grabbed each of the visitors by the windpipe.

"This one," Goldie went on, her beautiful face very motherly as she tousled Davey's hair, "is Jesse." The visitors now stood shoulder to shoulder as though waiting for a firing squad to turn up any minute.

"Yes, Mother," Davey quavered. He was a great actor even at that age.

"Do you notice any resemblance?" Goldie asked casually.

"*Resemblance?*" the visitors repeated nearly as one.

"Yes. But I can't call him by his daddy's *right* name . . . can I?"

The three split ranks, reformed magically into a triangular huddle.

"But I *will* see that he follows in his father's footsteps," Goldie went on. Of course this was all way above our heads, but we played it like professionals. I heard the name "Margoliese" and "rabbi" drift out of the huddle, accompanied by sharp little cries of alarm and confusion. Apparently Goldie heard too.

"Rabbi Margoliese . . ." she murmured dreamily.

Suddenly the visitors were right on us. We were relentlessly scrutinized and dissected. One woman stabbed a gloved finger at me and almost strangled on the name *Flaherty*.

"The dear man," Goldie said half aloud.

"Magistrate Flaherty?" another screamed.

"The dear, *dear* man," Goldie mused.

That did it.

"And these other two . . . who are their . . . their . . ."

"Fathers?" Goldie asked. "Well, I don't know that I should rightly tell you . . ."

"We insist . . . we must report back . . ."

"Well, there's two gentlemen in town who might not like it," Goldie said with a slight hesitation. "One's a big banker . . . the other . . ."

There was a commotion at the front door, followed by heavy footsteps. The huge form of Police Chief McCluskey loomed before the gathering. "I hurried down to see if you ladies needed any help," he said uncomfortably. He directed a nasty glance at Goldie.

"We were just on our way out," one visitor said. "Don't bother."

"I'll have Officer Kelley escort you out of the neighborhood." We followed them to the front door. We sat tight. Goldie leaned against the wall, smiling. Chief McCluskey came back, his face brick-red.

"Now what in hell are you up to, Goldie? What did you do to them snoopers?"

"Nothing, Harry. Sit down and I'll get you a drink." She glanced at us. "Tea."

"I don't want any goddam . . ." He glared at us. "Who are these little bastards?"

"Mine," Goldie answered. "All *mine!*"

"And you told them they're your'n?" He exhaled like a surfacing whale. "They'll sure as hell run you outa town on a rail now, Goldie!"

"No they won't." She put a cup and saucer before the police chief. "Matter of fact, they won't open their yaps."

"Whattya mean, they won't? Why them's local *society!*"

"They ain't going to accuse the town's chief magistrate, the head rabbi and Mr. John Dutton . . ."

"Bankers *Trust* Dutton?" the Chief said incredulously.

"And they didn't dare ask who the fourth little bastard's father might be," Goldie smiled, "because they were afraid I would name one of *their* husbands. . . ."

"Good God," Chief McCluskey sighed. Then he brightened. "Hey, Goldie . . . maybe you put an end to the A S and S." He slapped his knee. "B'jesus, maybe you did, at that!"

"Well, darlin', it's possible."

Suddenly the chief blew up again. His face was brickish once more.

"Now don't go darlinin' me, Goldie! Ya want me to lose

me job?" He turned on us. "And you little buggers go on home! What d'ye think yer folks will say if I tell thim I caught ya in a cathouse?"

Goldie then gave us each thirty cents while the chief watched the proceedings with disbelief. Everything was fine. We went our way after promising Goldie we would look in once in a while ... the idea being to take care of any extra ice cream, of course. I say everything was fine ... until that night at supper table. It was my dopey brother Frank who did it again. When Father asked casually what we had been doing that day, did we go for a swim ... ? Before I could stop him, Frank answered that we had spent the afternoon in a cathouse. Father choked on a swallow of coffee. Mother looked as though she had been hit by lightning.

"Goldie's cathouse," Frank elucidated, always helpful.

I didn't even *wait* to be told to leave the table and go up to my room. I marched up the steps with the same dignity I am sure the victims of the French Revolution exhibited as they climbed into the tumbrels on their way to decapitation.

CHAPTER XIII

Hobble Skirt

Now tell me why this skirt is tightly hobbled so...
And could I wear it and look neat, I'd like to know...

> *Hobble, hobble, hobble*
> *Is what we daily see,*
> *Hobble, hobble, hobble*
> *Which comes from old Paree...*
> *Which comes from old Paree.*
> *A fashion gown you see*
> *A fashion gown you see*
> *From ankle to the knee.*
> *Hobble, hobble, hobble.*

BREAKFAST WAS OVER and the dishes cleared. Mother scurried around the kitchen slamming pots and pans and talking in a half-murmur to herself, until Father came in—his glasses perched on the tip of his nose.

"Will ye stop frettin'? She's not comin' today so ye might as well accept the fact!"

"I must say you're not very concerned!"

"Concerned, is it?" Since Uncle Mike had gone, since Bess had lost the contest at the Orpheum, since the fake letter from the Klondike...months had passed. And my aunt's visits had become rarer and rarer. "Concerned, indeed! I've not had a Sunday's peace since himself took off like the Big Wind—and not much before."

I dried dishes in a desultory fashion—a penalty imposed by Mother for some minor infraction of house rules—and as I wiped, listened with a disinterested ear to my parents talk. Parents often gave me a sharp pain in the neck.

"It's that Mr. Fortesque person who worries me," Mother said.

"She's a good lass." Father poured a cup of coffee for himself. Mother grabbed a plate from my hand just as it wriggled out of my clutch.

"She's still a child."

"Bess is nineteen and will soon be bearin' wee ones."

Mother whirled on him. "They'd better be Mike's, by the grace of God and a gold ring!"

"Now what else would I be meanin'?" Father stepped

back, flushed, his coffee sloshing over into the saucer.

"It's my sister and I'll have nothing untoward happening to the girl!"

He took one more look at Mother's accusatory face, shook his head and decided to retreat with his coffee to the dining room. My chore finished, I made various noises and movements which signified that I was ready to leave for outdoor activities. Mother was unimpressed; the color was still high on her smooth cheeks.

"Bring in some wood," she ordered. Then, loud enough for Father to hear: "I haven't a thing to do this blessed day except bake cakes and pies for a bunch of hungry barbarians, and hang their clothes and pick up the papers, and worry myself sick about a silly girl!"

In the other room Father coughed, and I thought I heard a discreet "hah!" but I wasn't certain. I went to the shed and gathered the stubby chunks of firewood. By the time I returned Mother had simmered down and was fingering a bolt of satin on the kitchen table. I watched her closely, trying to gauge the strategic moment to ask for a reprieve. Mother inspected the cloth, pursed her lips and seemed to come to a momentous decision.

"Bring paper and envelope . . . and the pen and ink," she said to me.

Father brought his coffee cup back. "If I'm not bein' too nosey, who in the divil are ye writin' to?"

"Her Nibs." I handed Mother the writing paper. She glanced up at Father with the glimmer of a smile. "This will bring her down, or may the saints disown me!"

Father noticed the bolt of cloth. "Finery. A woman and her vanities . . ."

"Help me word it, Sandy?"

He frowned. "Dear Girl . . ." he began, hands behind his back ". . . it's with sisterly pleasure that I inform ye of a stroke of good fortune in the securin' of a hunk o' silk—"

"I'm not sending her a proclamation! . . . I should have better sense . . . I'll do it!"

Father looked at me and grinned. We heard the pen scratch across the paper for a while—then Mother smiled with satisfaction and read: "Dear Bess, please come to visit next week. I have some beautiful crêpe-back satin and about eighteen yards of soutache for a trim. Also pearl buttons and the latest Butterick modes. Miss Louella says she can come in for fittings so don't fail. Love."

Mother sealed the envelope and I decided this was the moment. "Mom—"

"Yes, you may go out," she said.

Crim-in-ees, I thought to myself, women—they can juggle yards of cloth and read a fellow's mind at the same time. Takes the pleasure out of life. I was in the back alley in five seconds flat.

The inducement of a new dress, I suppose, acted on Pretty Bess the same way that a wedge of banana pie might affect Frank, drawing him irresistibly to the source—or the way a batch of Mrs. Katz' warm, succulent kreplas (snitched by Davey for bargaining purposes) might compel me to part with anything I possessed . . . jackknife, marbles, even a pint of blood if that were the price. Anyhow, Pretty Bess turned up bright and early the following week, devil-may-care in manner and a bit offish with Mother. Toward me, however, she was her usual sweet self and she'd brought me a magnificent present: a new set of stereopticon slides of the Grand Canyon.

Wilting under my enthusiasm, Mother unlocked the bookcase in the parlor and brought out the stereoscope; at once I plunged into the magical, three dimensional pictures as she and Pretty Bess indulged in a preliminary sparring match. Frank trailed after me and nudged my elbow.

"Here," I said, "one look and make it fast!"

Mother had produced the bolt of satin and for a moment Pretty Bess' eyes glowed with excitement.

"It will make a beautiful hobble skirt," Mother said, "with the leg o' mutton sleeves and a ruche at the throat."

"Oh, it will!" Aunt Bess agreed. "And it's such a warm green . . . just my color too."

"You'll have to come down for fittings," Mother said pointedly, "for the next few weeks at least. Miss Louella doesn't work very fast."

Aunt Bess flushed. "I can't come next Sunday."

"And why not?"

"I have an important social obligation."

"My, my . . . we're getting very formal these days!"

Pretty Bess turned to me, an obvious hint that she didn't want to pursue the topic, but Mother had other ideas. After a measured period of silence, she asked, "Is it Mr. Fortesque?"

"As a matter of fact, it is!"

"I see."

Bess stroked the cloth, pushed it away, folded her hands in her lap. "Not when you say it that way, you don't! I've heard that tone before, Anne—but I'm not six now and you're not the sixteen-year-old big sister telling me what to wear and how to speak and brushing my hair in our bedroom at home—"

"Bess"—Mother's tone was gentle and patient—"Bess, what are you up to?"

Bess' mouth tightened. "I don't know what you're talking about I'm sure."

"Now don't you be using uppity airs with me, young lady!"

"I don't care to discuss the matter."

Pretty Bess peeled off her white gloves and smiled at me, nonchalantly but a little sadly, too, I thought. Mother sat down opposite my aunt. "Be reasonable, Bess. I want to have a serious talk with you—"

"And why didn't you have a serious talk with a certain individual and keep him from chasing fool's gold up in that terrible place?"

"It's not Mike who's heading for trouble, girl. . . ."

"I suppose *I* am!"

"That's what I intend to find out, here and now!"

They were getting started in earnest and I was just as glad when the front door opened and Father's head showed around the edge of the hall entrance. Frank was still glued to the stereoscope. I let him stay in the Grand Canyon and turned back to the women. Mother seemed annoyed at Father's interruption. He came in, grinned with pleasure when he saw Pretty Bess and kissed her cheek.

"Well, girl . . . 'tis a long time."

"Bess and I are talking," Mother said.

"Are ye now?" Her tone warned him. He frowned, slowly took off his jacket and equally slowly loosened the hard shirt collar. "Indeed?"

"Lady is worried about me," Bess said. She looked at Mother rather coldly and then turned back to Father with a flirtatious, joking manner. "It's a *serious talk* she wants with me. What do you think of that?"

Poor Father. Mother on one side, Pretty Bess on the other. He apparently decided caution was the best policy. "Well, we were kind o' worried, lass. Ye haven't been around much lately."

"Bess is quite taken up nowadays with *social obligations*."

Father, catching the import, scratched his reddish hair and nodded. The ice was getting thinner by the minute.

"Yes, Her Nibs is now in a social whirl with this *gentleman*, Mr. Fortesque, it seems," Mother said. "You remember, the one who says he wants to send herself here God knows where selling his music. . . . Do you hear me, Sandy?"

"And it's nobody's business but my own!" Bess said. "Is it, Sandy?"

Father looked vaguely toward the living room. "If ye'll excuse me . . . there's an article in the paper I want to finish. . . ."

Just then Frank came up for air, but I shoved a new slide in the viewer and his fists again clenched over the stereoscope. . . . The world could blow up with dynamite, the Delaware River could flood its banks, but as long as one or more of Frank's senses were seriously engaged . . . taste, smell, sight . . . he was literally out of this world.

"We might as well have an understanding right now!" Mother persisted. Bess lifted her chin defiantly—arms akimbo as if she were afraid she might let loose and throw convenient objects, as indeed, she had been known to do. Mother set her face muscles in the sidewise, down the nose, now-what-will-you-do-next attitude.

"Yes," my aunt said crisply, "we might as well!"

"You're a strongheaded girl . . . and don't be getting your back up till I've had my say. You've got a silly notion that Mike can't take care of himself, but that's not the whole reason you're scheming to quit your job and go traipsing around the country."

"Oh, isn't it, indeed! And have you been reading my diary again?"

"No, and I don't need to. I know you, Bess. Behind this whole scheme is the plain truth . . . you're stagestruck!"

I saw Bess wince. Her arms unlocked and she sat down and fumbled with the clasp of her purse. A little sullenly, voice suddenly uncertain, she asked, "What's wrong with that?"

Mother at once knelt beside the chair, arms warm and protective around her kid sister. "Bess, you *know* . . ." She handed her own white handkerchief to Bess, who promptly rolled it into a nervous ball. "All those loose women and the stage-door johnnies . . . it's not the way for a decent girl and nobody brought up as fine and wholesome as you would want to be part of that . . . that . . . that *fast* life. . . ."

Pretty Bess swallowed. Mother went to the sink and returned with a glass of water. But whatever Bess was going to say or whatever Mother expected her to say was interrupted by a light knock at the kitchen door.

"That will be Miss Louella," Mother said. "Right on time." She opened the door to admit Miss Louella, a faraway smile on her aged face and familiar carpetbag in her hand. Miss Louella swayed over to the sewing machine (Mother looked a bit askance, perhaps wondering if Miss Louella's recent conversion was already beginning to slip), took out her thimbles and thread ... and my aunt, I knew, was temporarily spared. Tempers were checked as the three women concentrated on the problem at hand, the creation of a finished dress from a bolt of brand-new green satin, all other worries pushed back into limbo. Mother pulled a kitchen chair into the middle of the floor, and my aunt stood on it while Miss Louella draped and measured, her mouth full of pins, her black bonnet bobbing up and down. She never took off her hat when she worked—it was the same one Nez had lifted off of her with ghostly deftness—and, looking back after all these years, I realize now that Miss Louella West was the first career woman I ever met.

Pretty Bess wanted a tight fit. Mother was dubious. Miss Louella was consulted and after much—and to me incomprehensible—discussion, a compromise was made. Flushed and busy, Mother looked up and spotted me.

"Why aren't you with the children?"

That annoyed me. They were my *gang*. Children, indeed! I frowned and stalked out.

Miss Louella might have been the only career woman we knew but Aunt Bess, despite the bribe of a new dress, was to stubbornly hold to her own schemes. When she came again to visit she was secretive, according to Mother ... and when she didn't come Father worried too.

"And what d'ye think she might be up to?" (It was some nervous-making time since her last visit.)

"I don't know, but I intend to find out!" Mother set the teapot down with a thump. Father frowned. No one spoke. Now and then, however, my father would look up, fork in hand and shake his head, absorbed in his own thoughts. Finally he turned to Mother, "Annie, I'm thinkin' it might be a good idea . . ."

She nodded her head toward me. "This one needs shoes again and the young one can do with a pair of corduroys. I do wish they made them out of iron. . . ." She glanced at Frank, startled. "Francis Richard! . . . now will you look at him!"

Up to his chin in food, Frank was totally oblivious to the talk around him. With one expert swipe, Mother reached over with a napkin and unearthed Frank's chubby face from beneath a layer of gravy.

The nature of their talk began to dawn on me. "Are we going to Philadelphia?"

Mother ignored me and addressed Father. "I'll take him to Strawbridge's tomorrow morning." I knew this meant me. "Then I'll drop over and see Bess before she quits work for the day."

Father nodded. "Sit up, lad, and eat right," he said to Frank. "Someday ye'll smother to death in a stew."

"I'll thank you not to call it a stew," Mother snapped. "It's potpie."

Her mind still on my Aunt Bess, Mother hardly heard Father's apology. "Yes," she said forcefully, "I'll find out what that girl is up to!" Mr. Fortesque's name was not mentioned, but even I felt it was hanging in the air.

Early the next morning, Mother deposited Frank with Mrs. Knowles. We went to the Square and boarded the trolley that, every twenty minutes, highballed between our town of Chester and the big city twelve miles to the north. I was excited. We rarely journeyed anywhere in those days, and a trip to Philadelphia was a big event.

When I had finally been shod in new thick-soled cleated shoes we left the department store and walked over to the big Five and Dime where my aunt worked. I imagined I was going to see her on some sort of stage, gowned and ravishing under a spotlight, while vast throngs listened to her sing, perhaps throwing bouquets at her feet. At least that's how I had seen it in the movies. But when we entered the Five and Dime we found my aunt simply by following the sound of a clear, strong voice through the crowd of Saturday morning shoppers. There was my aunt, beside an upright piano. She wore a high-necked white shirtwaist with a big blue silk bow. She looked the way she always looked—pretty, but certainly unspotlighted. A thin young man played the piano, his back to the listeners who stood three deep around the wooden railing. Pretty Bess held a song sheet in her hands but didn't bother to look at it while she sang. Her eyes were closed and there was a little smile on her lips.

"Kiss his picture in the frame . . . Call him all the sweetest names . . . Write him letters every day . . ." She sang, her long-lashed eyes closed, and I heard for the first time the full sweetness of her voice. When she came to our house she often sang, but not like *this*. Two men leaning on the rail straightened up and applauded vigorously when she finished, accompanied by a murmur of appreciation. A man in a pin-stripe suit, his eyes on Bess, whistled the tune, then broke into a toothy smile. My aunt held up the song sheet. "This is a new Lew Brown number . . . 'Please Don't Take My Lovin' Man Away'—" She saw us and stopped, startled. Then she nodded just as a woman leaned over and handed her another song sheet.

"Please sing this one, miss."

Pretty Bess knew most of the lyrics by heart. "I lost the

sunshine and roses...I lost the heavens of blue...I lost the beautiful rainbow...I lost the morning dew..."

When she finished the request number, someone from the crowd asked the title. " 'When I Lost You.' " Bess glanced at the title page. "Someone named Irving Berlin. He must be new, I guess."

She came over to us, ruffled my hair and whispered quickly, "Shopping? Ten more minutes and I'm free for lunch."

"Let's eat at Child's," Mother said. There was a faint disapproval on her face but we stayed anyway to watch Bess. She picked another song sheet off the rack near the piano, held it up and turned to the pianist. "I'm sure you'll enjoy this new one, ladies and gentlemen—'The Turkey Trot.' "

While we waited Pretty Bess sang, and sold, copies of the latest songs. In between her numbers the thin accompanist played the piano. There was laughter and applause twice as my aunt sang two brand new pieces: "Frankie and Johnny" and "I Want a Little Lovin' Sometime." I heard my mother make her reproving *tssk...tssk* sounds, but I enjoyed myself a lot. In fact, I was proud enough to bust wide open.

Some of the songs I knew. Pretty Bess would bring the latest ones with her when she visited and I would try to decipher the notes on the piano. She taught me to sing with a steady, sustained note..."From down here, down here!" ...and she would hold her hand over her flat stomach. I never produced anything but a chirping boy soprano but I did learn all the new songs: "Hold Me Just a Little Closer," "Waiting for the Robert E. Lee," "Roll Me Around Like a Hoop, My Dear," "The Sweetheart of Sigma Chi," "Dear Old Girl," "All Night Long," "I'm the Lonesomest Gal in Town," "I'll Sit Right on the Moon and Keep My Eye on You," "Love's Old Sweet Song," "Kitchy Koo," "The Hobble Skirt" and many, many others, some of them still beloved over a half century later.

Over lunch Mother and Aunt Bess fenced politely. Pretty Bess, overruling Mother, ordered a second dish of ice cream for me and Mother finally got to the point. "Bess, what *is* wrong? Surely you're not still—"

"I'm perfectly all right. I didn't come down Sunday because I had . . . an appointment."

"Ah."

Pretty Bess crumpled her napkin. "It was business."

My mother then adopted the identical tone she used often with me—a kind of gentle relentlessness to get at the bottom of things. "You're still my younger sister, Bess, I feel a responsibility . . . even if you sometimes seem to resent it. . . ."

Pretty Bess flushed, then got her back up. "You may as well know, I guess. I was going to wait until I was ready to go, then tell you—"

"Go? The saints preserve us—"

"I intend to leave in two weeks." She fingered her blue bow. "I'm going to find Mike, I can't wait any longer."

Mother gasped but before she could get a word in, Pretty Bess had reached across the table and clutched her hand. "He's sick . . . I worry something *horrible* has happened . . . I've had dreams . . . it's been too long since that last letter from him. There's no use trying to stop me, sis, it's all arranged. . . ."

Mother exhaled the breath she had held back. She took a sip of water, folded her gloves neatly, and spoke. "Young lady, suppose you start from the beginning."

"Mr. Fortesque has gotten me a job with his music publishing company . . ." She noted and rushed past the grim disapproval on Mother's face. "He's a gentleman," Bess said quickly, "regardless of what you think. He's going to introduce me to his boss Mr. Franklin, just like he promised, and they're arranging an . . ." she seemed to search for the word ". . . an *itinerary* for me. I'm to sing their latest songs during intermission at movie houses all the way across the country to Seattle."

"Indeed!" Ice in Mother's tone.

"Sis, he's a perfect gentleman."

"So you have told me. Twice. Well, I ask you, if he's such a gentleman, why doesn't *he* go to Alaska to find Mike?"

"This is business! I told you his boss was looking for a singer to promote their songs."

Mother sat back with a jerk. "When you get to Seattle what then?"

"I'm going to quit in Seattle." Bess lifted her chin defiantly. "Then I'm going on up to Fairbanks."

"Alone?"

"Yes, I'm not a child anymore!"

"All right. Fairbanks. And then?"

"I'll find Mike if I have to sing my way right up to the North Pole!"

My aunt looked at her lapel watch and rose. "I have to get back to work. Please . . . don't feel bad, sis," and then she hurried around the table and threw her arms around Mother, who sat there rigid and stared straight ahead. Pretty Bess then kissed me and left.

All the way back home, Mother was silent. I sensed this thing was beyond me and I'd better keep my mouth shut for a change. Besides, I knew she would tell Father about it the moment he came home from work. I wondered, though, why Pretty Bess had to go search for Uncle Mike who, after all, had been a war hero—although now and then it seemed even to me he was taking a long time to locate that barrel of gold!

CHAPTER XIV

Keep Away from the Fellow Who Owns an Automobile

Keep away from the fellow
who owns an automobile ...
He'll take you far in his motor car ...
Too darn far from your Ma and Pa ...
If his forty horsepower
goes sixty miles an hour ...
Say goodbye forever, goodbye forever.

Keep away from the fellow
who owns an automobile.

IT SEEMED TO ME that adults went out of their way to find things to worry about, while trouble had a way of finding innocent victims in my world of small fry. It was of an early evening shortly after coming back from seeing my Aunt Bess in Philadelphia that found me brooding in this profound fashion, disgruntled and sorry for myself, one mauled foot propped up on a chair on which Mother had placed a pillow. It was a foot salved, bandaged and temporarily out of commission, having been tramped on by a clumsy horse that refused to give me the right-of-way as I ran across the street clutching an apple that had dropped off a produce wagon, a prize I considered in the category of public domain.

Anyhow, my right foot was swollen It also throbbed naggingly. Frustration gripped me. I yearned mightily to be outside with my gang, for it was a warm night and in my moroseness I wanted to escape my parents, who were once again working themselves into a dither over Aunt Bess and her threatened trip to sell music—and locate Uncle Mike. Something dire was about to happen, said Mother, whom I knew from experience had uncanny instincts, easily on a par with those of a bird dog locating a quail that naively believes itself safely hidden in its camouflaged environment.

Eons later, or so it seemed that wearisome day, after we'd finished supper, Father undertook to lecture me sternly on the pitiable mental status of people, old or young, who foolishly expose themselves to unnecessary physical hazard, and had gone on to quote "that fellow Darwin" he seemed so hopped on—all this while Mother was safely out of earshot and busy upstairs—and he tried to convey the idea that one of the basic laws of Mankind, to paraphrase him, was recognition of the Need for Survival.

"Whin you git to college," he said, "ye'll learn the fittenest do the survivin', lad!"

"Aw, pop, I didn't see that darned horse!"

Father gave up. He muttered something to the effect that my uncle and I were, beyond doubt, atavistic throwbacks in the Mullen blood line.

Mother returned downstairs and unbandaged my foot for another inspection. I could never quite figure Mother's elusive reactions. That morning, she had run the gamut of emotions, uninhibited and contradictory emotions, to be sure. At the first shocked sight of my limping self, she'd swept me into her arms and almost smothered me with sympathy and affection. Despite the pain I felt this was a Heaven-sent opportunity and began to maneuver for a piece of the delicious Irish potato cake she had only a few minutes before removed from the ancient kitchen stove. But Mother had no sooner examined my foot, proclaimed it not serious, dabbed it with gobs of black ointment and bandaged it, than she turned on me like a fury. I was berated, warned, threatened and generally defamed. For the rest of the day I was given the silent treatment. Now, in the evening, she'd come full circle and was probing my bruised foot with compassion. Solicitous, matter-of-fact, as all get out.

"Thank goodness school's not begun," she murmured. "You'd have to stay home and miss classes."

I disagreed, of course. Bad timing. By me, school could remain missed forever.

Mother patted my head, then forgot me completely—or so I assumed—as she got out the ironing board and dumped an armful of freshly washed clothes on the table, partially covering Father's book under the light of the kerosene lamp. He grunted and shifted out of range.

"If I have to," she said to no one in particular, "I'll go to the Children's Aid Society."

"Now what would the Children's Aid Society have to do with a nag that steps on a lad's foot?" Father said. "Ye mean the SPCA!"

"*You* mean the Society for Prevention of Cruelty to Children, Mr. Know-It-All."

Father groaned and went back to his book.

"I was talking about Bess," Mother said.

He slammed the book down and took off his glasses.

"If I was a rich man," he said, "I'd have me a private den where I could pursue me intellectual studies and not be buffeted about by ceaseless blather."

Mother lifted the great flatiron from the stove, tested it with a finger and began to press. "Sandy, I practically raised Bess singlehanded. Even as a child, I remember she'd have this sly, secretive look in her face—and it never failed... whenever I spied it, Bess was just quietly sitting on a bunch of mischief. And now with all this talk of going off singing and—"

"She's love-sick for Mike, is all. Now I say let her talk about her grand schemes, she's not *done* anything so far... and meanwhile will ye try, jist try to be fair to the girl?"

Mother folded a pair of Father's long underwear. He wore wool longies on the job year round, even in hot weather. ("Keeps the damn foundry from creepin' right into me pores!")

"She's still seeing too much of this Fortesque person, for one thing! I told you he's offered her a job—"

"And nothin' will come of it, mark me words."

"Which way do you mean that?" she asked.

"Meanin'," Father aimed a finger at her, "the lass is not

interested in him, as ye well know . . . and while I'm admittin'
he's a sharp one, I'm sure it's her voice he's concerned with,
not her female charms—"

"Sandy," Mother ricocheted a swift glance to me. Her
eyes flashed. "You could be more careful!"

"Ahh . . ." He shook his head sadly, put his elbows on the
table and ran his fingers through his thin hair. In that exclamation, often used by my father, there was a world of meaning,
including: *Why can't a man be left in peace? Will the human
race ever reach a level only slightly above the apes? And
why can't problems be approached and considered with objective serenity?*

"I'm askin' jist one thing," he said quietly. "Will ye try
to be calm?" Mother watched him with a dead-level gaze and
let him talk without interruption. "A calm approach to the
problems of this life is the mark of intelligence! How d'ye
think I handle those skull-splittin' ironworkers—most of
thim furriners still bearin' the splinters in their shoes from
the gangplank they recently trod upon?"

"Hear the man talk!"

"And talk I will!" He made an effort and lowered his
voice to a tone more befitting a man who takes the falls and
foibles of life with unruffled wisdom. "If I let meself git
into a tizzy every occasion a little problem came up, Sam
Vulclain would not trust me with the responsibilities of
supervisin' the most important department of a company that
turns out the finest locomotives known to the world of en-
gineerin' science!"

Mother sighed and inspected a shirt of Frank's that she
had begun to iron. "The scamp," she murmured, "he's gotten
fruit stains all over it."

"That's all I'll be sayin' on the subject." Father picked up
his book again.

"From what I gather," Mother said crisply, "you've said
nothing that makes sense."

Again Father put aside his book, this time with slow deliberation. He cleared his throat:

> "In argument with men a woman ever
> Goes by the worst whatever be her
>   cause.
> For want of words, no doubt, or lack
>   of breath!"

Father glowered over his glasses. "John Milton, no less!" he said.

She banged the iron on the board, pushed it back and forth furiously. "Oh, Mother of God!"

"And another great mind had this to say about the need for calmness in the face o' trials and tribulations . . ."

"Jesus, Mary and Joseph!" Mother whispered.

Father was undeterred. He cleared his throat again.

> "Calm and serene he rides the furious
>   blast
> And, pleased the Almighty's orders to
>   perform,
> Rides in the whirlwind and directs the
>   storm."

"And that was none other than Addison himself!"

For a while there was only the soft thud of Mother's iron and the deep breathing of Father, who had gone back to his neglected pages. I contemplated my damaged foot and wondered suddenly, with a rush of excitement, if I could get away with a demand for crutches. *That* would be fun. But my thoughts, and those of the three of us, were interrupted by the unmistakable sound of the front door latch and the click of high heels in the hall. I perked up. Mother swung around from her laundry and Father snatched off his glasses. "Now that couldn't be . . ." he wondered aloud.

"Indeed it is! And this only Wednesday!" There was distinct alarm in Mother's words. "Oh, God, she can't be coming to say goodbye. . . ."

"Now, Annie . . . don't be leaping to conclusions."

Pale-faced, Mother untied her apron as Pretty Bess came in. She kissed us and in rapid, determined motions, took off her big-brimmed straw hat, jerked open the kitchen clothes closet and placed her hat and a silk parasol inside. All this without a word.

"Sit down, lass," Father beamed. " 'Tis a pleasure to see ye."

"It's not a bit pleasant I am tonight!" Bess said.

Mother didn't take her eyes off her sister but Father apparently saw nothing amiss because he rubbed his hands together and said pleasantly, "Lady and me . . . we've got a plan . . ."

My aunt produced a tiny handkerchief and dabbed her forehead. "I'd appreciate something cold to drink," she said to Mother.

Mother brought out a pitcher of lemonade and placed four glasses on the table, all the while pivoting her head to keep Pretty Bess in view. She had not yet said a word to her sister, not even "hello."

Father plunged happily on. "Now here's the idea," he said, "I have a bit o' money put aside . . ."

Mother poured the lemonade and passed me extra sugar.

". . . and ye can have it to go to a good singin' school!" Father said expansively. "What about that now?"

Pretty Bess seemed to have heard him for the first time. "Singing lessons?"

"Aye, lass. Ye've sich a fine voice, 'tis a shame not to take advantage of it!" He grinned. "It'll also be keepin' ye occupied nicely until Michael gets back . . ."

My aunt rose, kissed Father on his shiny forehead. "I'll

210 <Year of Our Lord

not be taking your hard-earned savings for any such thing! That money's been put aside for the house you'll buy some-day and . . ." she smiled at me ". . . for himself's education."

"Lass, will ye not be too hasty?"

"For heaven's sake, why do you all treat me like a child!" Bess flushed, and with a sudden irritated movement flopped down on the chair again and picked up her drink. There was a long, long pause. Father, finally accepting that something was wrong, kept shifting his gaze from Mother to Pretty Bess, his forehead creased in a deep frown.

I heard shouts outside, kids' voices, and I tried to peer through the dark. No good. Then, idly, I reached over and tugged at the window shade . . . raising . . . lowering . . . rais-ing . . . until the cord slipped from my clutch and the blind flew up with a wild, loud clatter.

"I wanted a bit of fresh air," Pretty Bess said slowly, "so I decided to take a trolley down and think things over."

We waited. Again a long pause. My aunt sipped her lemon-ade and wiped her lips. Mother carried the flatiron across the room and put it on the stove. When she came back to the table Aunt Bess was turning the lemonade glass around and around on the oilcloth, until at last Mother took it out of her hands.

Bess raised her long-lashed eyes and met Mother's patient silence. "Mr. Fortesque," she said flatly, "is *not* a gentleman after all!"

"I see," Mother murmured.

"And you needn't gloat about it!"

My father kept turning his attention from one to the other. "Now, whativer's the damn problem, let's not be flyin' off the handle!"

Both women acted as though he had evaporated into thin air. They seemed aware only of each other.

"Calm now! Everyone be reasonable," Father urged un-easily.

"Bess," Mother said, "all I'm asking, sister to sister, are you . . . are you *all right?*"

The tiny pendant Bess wore on her throat rose and fell and she twisted her handkerchief into an angry ball. "Oh, he was smooth as silk . . . telling me his boss was in town from New York and would I come up to the hotel—"

"*Who? What?*" Father, ignoring his own counsel, stumbled to his feet, his book dropping to the floor unheeded. He turned to Mother, eyes blazing. "Did that *scut* lay a hand on this girl?"

"You'd think," Pretty Bess tossed her head and spoke to Mother, "I didn't know a thing or two myself!"

"What in heaven's name *happened?*" Mother demanded.

Father shoved himself between the two. He waved his arms wildly. "Yes, what did he do . . . be quick about it! If you're meanin' what I think you're meanin' and if his intentions were what I'm thinkin' . . ."

"Well," said Pretty Bess, "he certainly turned out to be a snake in the grass."

"I'll break his damned back!" Father roared. "I'll crack his skull!"

"Now calm down, Sandy," Mother said.

"I'll give that scut a goin' over the likes never witnessed by mortal man!" Father's face was now bright red. He swung around and rushed to the hall closet.

"Now tell me what occurred . . . while himself throws a fit," Mother urged my aunt.

"It was right after work," Pretty Bess said, "and he came to the store and said Mr. Franklin was in town . . . that was last night . . ."

Father skidded back into the room. His coat hung from one arm, his hat jammed on his head. "Where does this blackguard live?" he shouted.

"He said—" my aunt addressed Mother—"Mr. Franklin would listen to me sing in his hotel suite. . . ."

"Never mind the preliminaries!" Father shoved the other arm into his coat. "Let's get to the heart of the thing! Don't spare me now—where the divil's me lid, Lady? I said—"

"Go ahead, Bess," Mother said calmly.

"It was the Bellevue-Stratford Hotel ..."

"Hmmm. Swank indeed!"

"*What's the scut's address?*"

"So I went," Pretty Bess said.

"Oh, ye did! The villain! Molester of innocence! When I'm finished with him, his own mother ..."

Mother reached over casually and took off Father's hat. She hung it directly in front of him on a chair.

"... won't recognize the scut!" He turned and headed toward the front door.

"Oh, he was smooth as cream!" Bess said.

Father came skidding back into the room. "Where's me damned hat?" He spied it on the chair, snatched it up and started off again. He came tearing back once more and halted before my young aunt. "I'm askin' onc't more ... where's this misbegotten creature live?"

"We drove in the fancy automobile of his to the hotel—" my aunt still spoke exclusively to Mother, "—and he was nice as pie on the way ... he said perhaps we ought to enjoy the ride a bit—that Mr. Franklin wouldn't mind waiting!"

"Now hear me ..." Father began pounding the table, his features brick-colored apoplectic.

Mother again divested him of the hat, hung it on the chair.

"But I said I was afraid of automobiles ... we shouldn't keep Mr. Franklin waiting, and the instant we walked into the suite," Pretty Bess went on, "I knew Mr. Franklin wasn't coming. ..."

"That does it!" Father stalked in a tight circle around Mother and for the third time rushed off.

"There was a table set ... champagne and those little black fish eggs ..."

Father came tearing back again. "Where's me damned hat?"

"Caviar," Mother said.

"Cavy-who?" my father shouted. He saw his headpiece, grabbed it furiously and put it on.

"Fish eggs..." Mother turned to him. "The kind the rich like."

"What in hell's all this fish stuff!" Father shook a wrathful finger under Pretty Bess' nose, which was uptilted in her own maidenly anger, and bellowed, "*What is this man's address!*"

Mother quietly relieved him of his hat once more while Father waited for the words that would make him an avenging St. George.

"And there was a great bouquet of roses..." Bess said.

"Ahhh..." Father breathed. "It'll be a shambles sich as Nature herself can't match whin I'm through with him!"

"So I says to him, 'Mr. Fortesque, I'll be thanking you to unlock that door...'"

"He made you prisoner!" Father whirled, began to rush to the front door, hit the archway and almost fell. He clapped a hand to his head and shouted. "Where's that damned hat!"

"Here," Mother said solemnly.

He put it on and closed his eyes, addressing the ceiling. "I'm goin' out of me damned mind!"

Mother retrieved the hat again, this time she placed it on the seat of the chair. Father opened his eyes and shoved his face right into my aunt's. "For the last time, *Where does this violator of womanhood live?!*"

"Oh, Sandy, sit down," Mother commanded.

"Sit down, she says!"

Pretty Bess rose and threw her arms around Father. "The poor man really believes I've been done in," she said, "Sandy, nothing happened!"

Father sat in sudden collapse on the chair and, of course,

on his hat. With an anguished bellow he jumped up and deliberately kicked the hat across the room.

"The fit's over," Mother announced. "You were saying, Bess . . . you're all right?"

"Of course I'm all right. I mean about what *some* people are apparently thinking . . . I slapped his face, told him I'd scream . . . and then I walked out."

Father ran his hands through his hair.

"Mother of God . . . women . . ." He picked up his crumpled hat, looked at it sadly. "Women . . . women! . . ."

CHAPTER XV

The Miner's Dream

The miner when he goes to sleep
soon begins to snore,
Dreams about his friends at home
whom he may see no more,
A lonely wife or sister dear
he may have left behind,
Perhaps a father old and gray,
A mother good and kind......

As THE OPENING of school approached, my gang and I lapsed into a slow coma, and on the crisp morning when we actually set off for the red-brick building on Water Street, Hank, Moisha, Nez, and I—all fourth grades-men—met at the street corner, lips bloodless, eyes blank, and walked off together very much like lemmings that are purported to make annual migrations to oblivion.

But little Davey, as it turned out, had more guts than his elders: he simply disappeared that fateful eight o'clock and was later picked up on the highway between Chester and Philadelphia by curious police who wondered what in the world a seven-year-old runt like that had in mind as he walked the highway carrying a bundle on his shoulder that was loaded with kreplas, marbles, a cigarette picture-card of Annette Kellerman in a daring one-piece bathing suit, a slingshot, and a few odds and ends of clothing. He was forthwith returned to his home and the next day Mrs. Katz personally escorted him to his class. (The fact that my gang went on in life to hold various positions of accomplishment and dignity doesn't negate the truth that back in our youth we were not what might be considered honor students. All learning we received was the result of relentless, selfless and saintlike sacrifice on the part of our harassed teachers.)

However devastating the inauguration of each new school term, we managed in time to recover from our comatose condition and eventually to take accustomed interest in Life around us. Deep in our collective hearts I think we knew that school was as inevitable as baths and periodic sore throats.

We had to accept the routine of the classroom because that was the way the world was, and no getting around it. So for a few months we would rebel valiantly against education and then, when we were resigned and disciplined, the late autumn foliage was already a deep russet and the air had a wild tang that made it good to breathe and sharp to taste.

It was also at this time in the year of our Lord 1912 that I very much missed Uncle Mike—in my fashion perhaps as much as Pretty Bess, now long-suffering and languishing, missed him.

Because Uncle Mike, who was all of thirty, had always meant love of outdoors to me, and I now recalled how, for example, he used to drop by on a brisk autumn day and take me for a long hike into the flamboyant Pennsylvania countryside. He loved to stride along a wagon-rutted road, muffler around his neck, big hands jammed into his coat, and tell me of the greatness of Life, particularly those greatnesses he, personally, had accomplished. On these memorable hikes I would carry his canvas-covered metal canteen imprinted with a huge "U.S." in black letters and we would spot a spring somewhere along the road and fill it with cold crystal-clear water and then we would go on our way until Uncle Mike would say, "We'll bivouac here, lad," and we would sit, perhaps under a tree beside the road, and eat a wonderful baked potato or a thick sandwich and take turns drinking from the canteen.

No, excursions into the countryside were just not the same without Mike. The season of the year I loved best was empty without his hearty voice and his rich, Irish exuberance.

I had stopped pestering my folks about Uncle Mike's lack of correspondence to us and Mother cautioned me strongly not to raise the question in front of Pretty Bess, whom, I saw without having it pointed out to me, was subdued these days, her lovely face thinner.

"It's thim voice lessons," Father decided. "What with the

store and the voice trainin', the lass works too hard. Now it's an inevitable law that labor-and-no-fun will take its toll o' good spirits, Lady!"

"Hard work never hurt a living soul!" Mother said. "No, Sandy. It's the *not knowing* that does it."

When she visited us, betrayed by Mr. Fortesque, abandoned by Uncle Mike, Bess would go into the parlor, close the folding doors and spend long hours playing the piano and singing. "It's more like a keening," Mother said more than once to my father.

Mother outdid herself during that time, shopping for new dress fabrics and having Miss Louella in to sew as Pretty Bess stood straight and patient with a faraway look in her big eyes while Mother and Miss Louella measured, pinned and fluttered over the new costumes. Meals became heavier on Bess' favorite dishes—pot roast and potatoes and mince pie—and she performed the remarkable feat of eating, chatting and teasing me or Frank while she preserved at the same time her air of unnatural, even ominous calm. There were no more arguments in our house. It was strangely peaceful— even Father seemed edgy with such an excess of calm—and we all just seemed to wait. For what, none of us quite knew.

One glorious November twilight I rushed out of the house, swinging my beat-up hockey stick, en route to find the gang. I had cut back through the alley when I saw the tramp. Mother had often warned Frank and me about tramps. "Treat them politely," she had admonished, "but never go anywhere with them. Remember that!"

Tramps were not uncommon in our town. Generally they wore old clothes, carried bundles tied with rope, and some— like the one standing in the alley now—were in need of a shave. I hesitated. The alley was narrow. The tramp walked toward me. His great beard hung to his chest, black and matted. He wore an enormous fleece-lined mackinaw, all stained, and his head was covered with a crumpled felt hat, dark with soot. I wanted to run but I didn't want to be a coward. I was afraid. The tramp came up to me, his eyes fixed hard on my face. I waited.

"How are ye, Gasoon?"

I would have known that voice anywhere in the world! I gulped and was dumb.

"So ye don't recognize yer uncle, Gasoon?" He put his hand on my shoulder. "Ah, now, 'tis perhaps this fuzz on me face, eh?"

"Uncle Mike!" I managed to squeak. "Hey, where's the gold mine?"

He laughed, the same rich laughter, although his hands looked like yellow bones. "I'll be tellin' ye all about the gold mine soon's ye tell *me* somethin'."

I began to get over my shock. "Sure, Uncle Mike!"

"Well, now"—he winked—"is himself at home?"

"Pop just got home from work."

"Ah now, and d'ye think ye could do me a favor?"

"Sure . . . sure!"

"Could ye go upstairs . . . soft as a wee kitten, and kinda lay hands on yer father's razor and brush . . . perhaps a cake of soap?" He forestalled my questions . . . "All right, Gasoon, let's save the why's and how's and whin's till later, like a good lad, eh?"

"I can do it, and pop wouldn't know . . . sure!"

"Now mind ye, not a word I'm here yet. Agreed?'"

I snitched Father's straight razor, brush and soap, and tore back to the alley. "Now where can a man find a place to tidy up?" he asked.

"Mr. Armitage shaves right in his office over the stable," I offered breathlessly. There were a million things I wanted to ask as I followed Uncle Mike, who headed, with a slow tired tread, toward the barn. "He's got hot water, too."

Old Man Armitage smoked his foul cigar and watched in tactful silence as Uncle Mike sheared off some eight months' of black beard. Now and then he groaned, as if it were painful, and I hopped from one foot to another bursting with questions I didn't dare ask until my uncle gave me the go-ahead. His face was much thinner once the beard was off—downright bony—and his eyes were sunk deep behind his brows. Old Man Armitage put down his cigar and filled a huge wooden tub with hot water. "Try that," he said. "Soak as long as you like."

There was nothing Uncle Mike could do about a haircut, but when he took off his ragged apparel he didn't look like a tramp anymore. The old man gave him a towel to dry himself. My uncle thanked Mr. Armitage, and we set off for the house.

As we walked, he hardly seemed to hear my chatter.

"Eh, lad? Later . . . later . . . tell me, how's Pretty Bess?"

We entered the house by the back door. Plates were set for supper and Father was already in his chair at the head of the table. Mother, her back to the entrance, was dishing up a great bowl of spareribs and sauerkraut. The door banged. Father glanced up and uttered a choked sound.

Mother turned around. "The Virgin bless us!" The spoon dropped and she threw her arms around my uncle. "Mike . . . Mike Mullen!"

Father stood up, fiddled with his belt, while Mother exclaimed and blew her nose.

"Michael," he said quietly. He held out his hand. "How are ye, lad?"

They stood there, my father and uncle, looking at each other and pumping their clasped hands up and down, up and down, and not a word said except Father's repeated "how are ye, lad? how *are* ye?"

Frank came in. He sniffed the fragrant kitchen odor and said, "Hello, Uncle Mike," just as though my uncle had been around all the time. He then sat down to table, ready for the important business at hand. Mother picked up her spoon. Father shoved my uncle into a chair.

"Git another settin' for Michael, Lady!" he said. "The man's famished. Lookit the poor skin and bones of him!"

"Well now"—Uncle Mike grinned—"the subject bein' mentioned, I'll not be denyin' I could do with a snack or two." He ran a hand over his face, and I thought he looked awfully tired. "It's not much sleep I've had these many weeks."

"Ye'll bed down here until sich time as yer set," Father said. "We have more than enough room—"

"No, Sandy, only fer the night. I'll be gettin' back up to Philly tomorrow."

Father started to protest but Mother shook her head in warning and he quickly gave it up. I sat down next to Frank and pulled the bread out of his reach. Uncle Mike turned to Mother, and there hung in the air between them the unspoken, most important matter of all.

"Bess is fine," Mother said. "She's missed you, Mike." She dabbed her eyes with the apron.

"All right, now," Father said, "let the man have his grub."

No one paid me any attention. I took a deep breath. "Hey, Uncle Mike!" I got attention. "Where's the barrel of gold?"

"Will everyone let the man alone?" Father said testily. "Not a word now till he's properly fed!"

There began a clatter of knives and forks . . . meat was passed, and bread, and salt, and for once in his life Frank was up against stiff competition in the victuals department. Uncle Mike ate three helpings of spareribs, two of kraut, and when the bread pudding was consumed he sat back and let forth a rumbling belch.

"Ah, 'tis good to taste yer cookin' again, Lady!" he said. "Ye'll pardon me if I show it?"

Mother smiled with pleasure and Uncle Mike turned to

me, inhaling comfortably. "Now, Gasoon, about that barrel o' gold . . ."

"There's no need to explain a thing," Father said.

"There is, indeed, and I might as well have it over with."

"Where d'ja leave it?" I demanded.

"Did you come back just like that . . . no belongings?" Mother interrupted.

"I am as ye see me, Lady."

"Ye're taller than me," Father said, "but I have a suit and shirt ye can have."

"I appreciate that, Sandy, but dammit, man—"

"How about the barrel of gold?" I was getting shoved out of the picture.

"Ye'd better tell the lad," Father said quietly.

Uncle Mike reached into his pocket and pulled out what looked like a piece of molten metal about the size of a large walnut kernel. He placed it near my plate. "It's a nugget o' gold, Gasoon," he said, "and it's sorry I am I couldn't bring back a barrel of it."

Father took it from me and tried to estimate the weight. "How did ye travel back?" he asked Uncle Mike. "By the rods, I'll wager, from the looks of ye! And how much would ye say this bit o' metal is worth?"

"Sure, I could of got a bit of change fer it . . ."

"Why in hell didn't ye . . . and come home decently?" Father exploded.

"Now, Sandy," Mother warned. "Not tonight!"

"Himself has a point there, Lady." Uncle Mike turned to me. "Ye can call it false pride or what not, Gasoon . . . but I wanted to bring home at least a small chunk o' the Klondike after all me fine talk and tribulations . . . ."

Then, and for the only time I ever remember, I saw Uncle Mike lose his cocky assurance. "The whole lot of ye are too good fer the likes o' me," he said. His deep voice wavered.

"No, Sandy, I want ye to hear me out...fer I'm the mule-headed kind who might never have the nerve to say it again. I'm a scatterbrained fool who ain't got the sense God endowed him with...I have caused a lot o' worry to all concerned...."

"I'll not have ye talk that way!" Father roared.

"Ah, but I will! I've got it comin'. I ought to have me head examined and me backside kicked hard!"

Father almost upset the table as he rushed around to Uncle Mike and shook him by the shoulders. "Ye'll not berate yerself, Michael!"

"Let me say me say, dammit!"

"Sure, I think as much o' ye as I do me own ones here..." Father swept his arm to include Mother, Frank and myself "...and never has a man loved his wife and wee ones more than I do, do ye hear? So enough o' that kind o' nonsense!" He went back to his place and swallowed some coffee. "And while we're openin' our hearts and exposin' 'em, let me say this and I'll not repeat it again..."

He clenched a fist and rubbed it on the table, his chin on his chest. "Now jist be patient...let me find the words..."

Uncle Mike was silent. Mother pulled the sugar bowl away from Frank. Albert scratched under the stove.

"Well, Michael"—Father finally brought it out—"it's jist this! Ye *should* o' did what ye did!"

"How's that again?" Uncle Mike said.

"I admire the gumption o' ye, man!"

"Well, I'll be damned!"

"I'm glad ye stood on yer hind legs and told me to go to hell."

"I'll be double damned!"

"Himself is just saying what I knew all along," Mother said. "He was proud of you, Mike, even though he felt it was a fool's journey."

"The woman is right. I was agin the whole venture," Father nodded. "And I'm still agin such foolishness. Why man, the world's settlin' down . . . the frontier's gone . . ."

"Sandy!"

"I was only about to say—"

"Yes, dear," she said, "but you have the cart before the horse. Mike's *back*, he's not about to leave!"

A strange feeling permeated all seventy pounds of me. It was the peculiar vivid sensation you sometimes get as a youngster, and lose later in life, that overwhelms you with a special prickly sense of *knowing* . . . and however momentary the experience, you're almost floored with the acuteness of the recognition. At that moment I saw or *felt* a new Father with a new understanding. *That's* my father, I thought. He loves my uncle! He had defended him. He had not lashed out and said '*Michael you have failed, you have caused us sorrow, you have been an aimless, unsuccessful fool.*' These words were what I had expected. Instead he had said to Uncle Mike, *You did what you wanted to do and you let no one stand in your way.*

Somewhere in a busy year, the stick-in-the-mud had grown to a new stature.

And maybe my Uncle Mike saw Father in a different way too, because he wagged his shaggy head and said, "B'jesus, if I live to be a hundred, Sandy, I'll niver forget this minute. Jis whin I was flat and needed a helpin' word, ye gave it to me!"

There followed a silence. Everybody, it seemed, including me, needed a few moments' grace to catch themselves up with events.

And then it hit me with the impact of a sledge! The nugget on the table was the sum total of Uncle Mike's great adventure. There was not, nor would there ever be, a "barrel o' gold"! Pretty Bess wouldn't wear sables and ride around in a glittering Pierce Arrow. And my gang wouldn't, in winters to come, fly over snowy roads covered with ermine blankets....

"Buck up, lad," Father said loudly. "Gold or no gold, yer Uncle Mike's back with us."

"Yes, sir."

"Don't be feelin' bad, Gasoon." Uncle Mike wrapped a big arm around me and included us all in his grin. "I'm thinkin' there's plenty of treasure right under our noses!"

"Enough of this hot air!" Father said. "How about a nip for celebration?"

He brought out the whiskey and while the men drank "a nip" Mother announced she would go over to the livery stable to call Pretty Bess. At once, Uncle Mike jumped up.

"B'jesus now Lady, not so fast! I don't wan't the darlin' girl to see me lookin' like the last wilted rose o' summer."

"We'll drape some decent clothes on yer back," Father said. "Niver fear, Mike ... ye'll be garbed head-to-foot in me best!"

An hour and several nips later, Pretty Bess rushed into the house. Uncle Mike stood up when she entered. Wordless, a bit bony and in bad need of tonsorial attention. Bess paused at the hall archway, and I'm sure she saw no one in the room except my uncle. A puzzled expression flashed across her eyes.

"Mike," she said, "you've grown!"

My mother giggled. Uncle Mike blushed and tugged at the sleeves of Father's suit jacket, vainly trying to cover three inches of exposed wrists. The trousers, likewise, were several inches too short. Flustered, he said, "Now, don't be laughin' at me, girl. It's *himself's* suit I have on me back!"

Pretty Bess dropped her parasol on the floor and flew, yes, *flew*, to my uncle's arms. "Oh, you big fool! Mike ..." she said "... Mike!"

Mother opened the doors of the parlor. Quietly and with

efficiency she nailed Father with a glance, turned me about and faced me toward the kitchen. "Go out and play," she said.

Then she shepherded my uncle and aunt into the parlor and closed the big doors. "Well, that's that, praise God!"

"Amen," Father smiled.

And that's the way it was—cross my heart!

Epilogue

WHAT HAPPENED to them? My family has departed this vale
of tears and laughter—I don't know about the Katz ménage
because we moved out of that boisterous (and really happy)
neighborhood before the outbreak of World War I in 1914.

It was a time almost without precedent. Consider: The last
great conflict had ended forty-three years before and had
become a blurred memory, but the towns were full of Civil
War veterans in the age brackets of sixty to seventy. Old
man Armitage fought at Chickamauga. Town Police Chief
McCluskey was left for dead at Gettysburg. It was a time
when a Union cavalryman leaned down from his horse and let
me handle his sword. It was a time when the Past touched the
Future.

My parents' generation grew up in an atmosphere of opti-
mism. The nation was explosive with energy, growth and
confidence. World War I was years off. There was work to
be had, vast areas of the land still to be explored or settled.
You took home your full week's wage or salary. There were
no income taxes—no taxes at all. It was, I think, a healthy
interim. You *might* have died younger because medical science hadn't come up with antibiotics or heart and kidney
transplants. Pneumonia was a bigger threat than cancer. Nowadays, you can be surgically remade, or antibiotically saved

so that you can spend your declining years on a park bench or forgotten in a home for the aged.

There was no television, not even radio, and movies were a manic, jerky affair in Nickelodeons seating at most a hundred souls.

Narcotics were not hawked openly on street corners; sex was a private and beautiful matter, deviants were around, to be sure, but they did not flaunt their preferences, violence-dispensing muggers were unheard of.

There were jobs, plentiful food, half the world wasn't hungry while the other half feared they might drop the Big One any day now—and the biggest White House scandal occurred when they caught an obese President pinching little girls' fannies.

Lest the reader think this fellow is a prude, a square, I say I am not. But I *am* fed up with self-appointed critics of the good old days who cry loudly and frequently that this nation never enjoyed such times, that they never happened. Interestingly, these declaimers, whether they use the written word, films or television, are generally of the ripe old ages of twenty-five to thirty-one.

They were not only good old days, the future was wide open and inviting. If you didn't like wrestling beer kegs you could take off for the Klondike, return a failure and be welcomed with love and respect. It was a wonderful time.

Cross my heart, hope to spit!